# More Math Games & Activities

## from around the

# World

# More Math Games & Activities

## from around the

# World

# Claudia Zaslavsky

CHICAGO
REVIEW
PRESS

**Library of Congress Cataloging-in-Publication Data**
Zaslavsky, Claudia.
More math games and activities from around the world / Claudia Zaslavsky.— 1st ed.
    p. cm.
    Summary: Presents games and other activities from different countries and cultures
that teach a variety of basic mathematical concepts.
Includes bibliographical references.
    ISBN 1-55652-501-X
    1. Mathematical recreations—Juvenile literature. [1. Mathematical
recreations. 2. Games.]  I. Title.

QA95.Z37 2003
793.7′4—dc21

                                                                      2003004380

Cover design: Mel Kupfer

First edition
Published by Chicago Review Press, Incorporated
814 North Franklin Street
Chicago, Illinois 60610
ISBN 1-55652-501-X
Printed in the United States of America
5 4 3 2 1

To the people of the world, with my profound wish for a peaceful tomorrow and bright future for all.

# Contents

## ACKNOWLEDGMENTS

I want to thank the many educators and authors who shared their
expertise to make this book possible. Their books and articles are
listed in the Bibliography. My husband, Sam Zaslavsky, took
all the photographs and helped in many other ways. Thanks to J. Weston Walch,
Princeton U. P., and Marcia Ascher for permission to publish. Also thanks to
Mr. and Ms. Abelson, Ms. Schnipper, and Mr. Smith for use of their photographs,
and Dr. Crowe and Dr. Gerdes for use of their drawings. I take full
responsibility for any errors or lack of clarity.

# Introduction

## A NOTE TO PARENTS, TEACHERS, AND CAREGIVERS

This book is a follow-up to my 1998 volume *Math Games and Activities from Around the World*, also published by Chicago Review Press. You may ask: Why encourage children to play games when there is so much math to be learned? That is exactly why! In the course of engaging in these fun activities, children utilize many important skills. They calculate, measure, and solve problems. They hone their abilities in geometry and in the recognition of patterns. Most of all, they learn to think critically.

Children who are uninterested in or bored by traditional math lessons are willing to persevere to find solutions to problems posed in a challenging game format. The activities are open-ended; kids can engage with them as far as their interests and abilities carry them. Several different versions of some games and activities are presented so that children can gain wide experience with the relevant concepts. Furthermore, children learn about some aspects of mathematics that are not included in the school curriculum, such as networks (graph theory) and fractals.

These games and activities are appropriate for children aged nine and up, although some will appeal to younger children and others may challenge adults. Many of the projects are suited to collaboration between adults and children, or for cooperative groups of students. Each game and activity concludes with suggestions for further thought and research.

Activities may be chosen to fit into the math curriculum or to relate to topics in language arts, social studies, science, or fine arts. Refer to the chart (page 158) for the mathematical and nonmathematical content of each activity. Readers may find answers to some problems on pages 153 to 154. Reproducible pages of square and triangular (isometric) graph paper appear on pages 150 and 151.

According to the National Council of Teachers of Mathematics document, *Principles and Standards for School Mathematics*, published in 2000: "Mathematics is one of the greatest cultural and intellectual achievements of humankind, and citizens should develop an appreciation and understanding of that great achievement, including its aesthetic and recreational aspects" (page 4).

Through these games and activities, children learn to appreciate the history and culture of many societies. This book integrates math, history, art, literature, and world cultures to make math exciting for all children.

## A NOTE TO KIDS

This book presents more games and activities from around the world, a follow-up to my *Math Games and Activities from Around the World*. Here you will find more versions of three-in-a-row games and Mankala, old games going back hundreds and thousands of years to Africa, as well as less familiar games from many lands. Children in Mongolia, in the Far East of Asia, play games similar to Tic-Tac-Toe on several kinds of boards. Kids in other parts of Asia pretend that tigers eat lambs in their board games.

Other activities deal with your own environment and beliefs. How can you save water and precious materials? Do you think that some numbers are more lucky than others? You will find out why magic squares are magic. You will learn to make beautiful designs and copy some of the lovely patterns in quilts and other objects, and perhaps read books about these designs.

All these games and activities use math. Some of the math is different from math you learn in school, ideas like fractals in Native American baskets and networks from West Africa and India. Read the hints and suggestions, and don't give up. Perhaps you will want to discuss the problems with your friends or a grown-up. A few of the activities have answers in the back of the book. Most are self-checking. You can decide whether your answer makes sense. If it doesn't, you will have the satisfaction of finding the reason, even if it takes a while.

Most of the board games are for two players or teams. You can also work out strategy by playing the games by yourself. Pretend that you are two people and play both sides of the board. Of course, everyone likes to win. But if one player is always the winner, the other player is always the loser and may give up. Help your opponent to learn better strategies, and the game will become more interesting for you. Winning isn't everything!

I hope you and your friends have fun with this book!

# More Math Games & Activities

from around the

# World

# ① Three-in-a-Row Games

**I**n most parts of the world people play some form of three-in-a-row games. The object of the game is to place your three markers in a row on the game board. You have probably played Tic-Tac-Toe. Many of these games are more complicated than Tic-Tac-Toe.

All the games are for two players, sometimes for two teams. You can also play them by yourself. Pretend that you are two people, and play on both sides of the board. This is a good way to learn a new game, or to work out the fine points of strategy, as though you were solving a puzzle.

The games in this chapter gradually become more complicated. They begin with a simple game called Nine Holes from England, with three counters for each player. As you go through the chapter, the games will require more counters. Finally you come to Murabaraba from southern Africa, in which each player starts with 12 counters. Of course, the game board also becomes more complex as you go from one game to the next. In the last activity you will analyze the connection between the type of game board and the number of counters.

These games call for two kinds of counters or markers. Kings and princes used to play with beautiful pieces made of gold and ivory. Ordinary people used stones or seeds, or peeled and unpeeled twigs. You can also use red and black checkers, or two kinds of coins, or make your own special counters.

Game boards for three-in-a-row games have been found scratched in the stones of the rooftop of an ancient Egyptian temple built 3,300 years ago, and in several other ancient sites. The games in this book come from many parts of the world. Look up these places on a map or globe.

Wherever you might travel, you will probably find that people play some version of these games. Although you may not be able to speak their languages, you can make friends all over the world with three-in-a-row games.

## TIPS TO THREE-IN-A-ROW FUN

Three-in-a-row games require several types of game boards. You will probably want boards that will last for a while. Draw the lines neatly with a ruler on paper, and glue the paper to cardboard or mat board. It's a good idea to make a pattern on a sheet of scratch paper first.

Some people play games just to win and they get upset when they lose. Playing a game should be fun. When one player always wins, the other player must always lose, and may give up after a while. Helping an opponent to improve his or her skills makes the game more interesting for both players.

Each player should have an equal chance of winning. In some games the first player to move is more likely to win. Players should take turns going first in this type of game.

You may want to vary the games. A slight change in the rules, or in the shape of the game board, or in the number of counters may call for an entirely different strategy. Just be sure that both players agree on the new rules before the game starts.

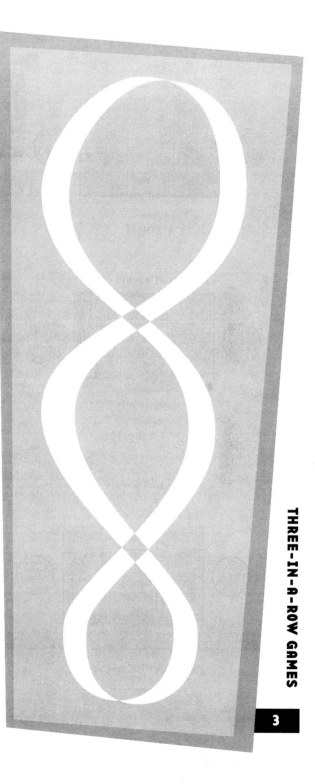

# Nine Holes from England

**N**ine Holes is one of the simplest of all the three-in-a-row games. Very young children can learn to play it. I read in a book on African games that four-year-olds in some parts of Africa like to play games similar to Nine Holes. They learn to take turns and to think about their moves. They also learn that there is no point in getting upset when they lose a game. Nine Holes is a good introduction to Tic-Tac-Toe and other three-in-a-row games.

Long before anyone had heard of Tic-Tac-Toe, people were playing Nine Holes. It was a favorite among the boys who herded sheep and cattle. While the animals were feeding in the pastures, two boys would agree to draw the game board on the ground. They would dig three rows of holes, three holes in each row. They would gather three stones of one kind and three of another kind, and be ready to play.

The seventeenth-century English poet Michael Drayton described the scene:

**The unhappy wags, which let their cattle stray,
At Nine Holes on the heath whilst they together play.**

Some of these "unhappy wags" invented strange rules for the game. On the Salisbury Plain, in southern England, the counters were not stones, but wooden pegs stuck into the earth. The players had to get down on the ground and pull out the pegs with their teeth!

In many old English churches one can find sets of holes or lines for three-in-a-row games. Centuries ago the few boys who were lucky enough to go to school in England usually attended church schools. The boring lessons seemed to go on forever, and the boys were often tempted to sneak in a quick game of Nine Holes.

Even grown-ups were guilty of playing games when they should have been attending to the Sunday sermon. An English court record for the year 1699 tells of two men who were punished for playing Nine Holes during church services.

The religious beliefs of the New England colonists did not permit gambling or games played with dice or cards. Children who spent time in play of any kind were warned: "Satan finds some mischief still for idle hands to do." Still, both grown-ups and children in the New England colonies did play Nine Holes, as well as more complicated three-in-a-row games like Nine Men's Morris and Twelve Men's Morris, in which each player had either nine or twelve counters.

Children in other countries play games that have the same rules as Nine Holes, but different names. Here are some of them:

| Country | Game Names |
| --- | --- |
| Arabic-speaking countries | Dris ath-tha-latha |
| Germany | Nulochen and Neun Locher |
| Japan | San-noku-narabe |
| The Netherlands | Dreisticken |
| Nigeria | Akidada |

## MATERIALS

- Sheet of unlined paper, at least 8 inches (20 cm) square
- Pencil
- Ruler
- Colored markers or crayons
- Scissors
- Glue
- Piece of cardboard, at least 9 inches (22.5 cm) square
- Three counters for each player, of two different kinds (beans, buttons, checkers, or coins)

## DRAWING THE GAME BOARD

**1.** On the sheet of paper, draw a square that measures 6 inches (15 cm) on each side.

**2.** Draw lines that connect the midpoints, or middles, of the opposite sides.

**3.** Use a marker or crayon to mark the nine points where the lines meet, as shown in the diagram. **Figure 1**

**4.** Glue the paper to the cardboard and decorate your game board. You will want to use it over and over again.

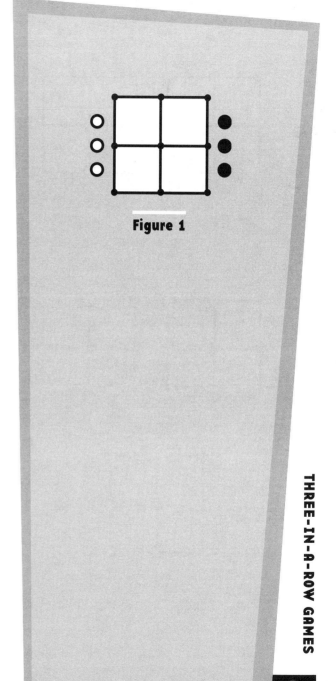

**Figure 1**

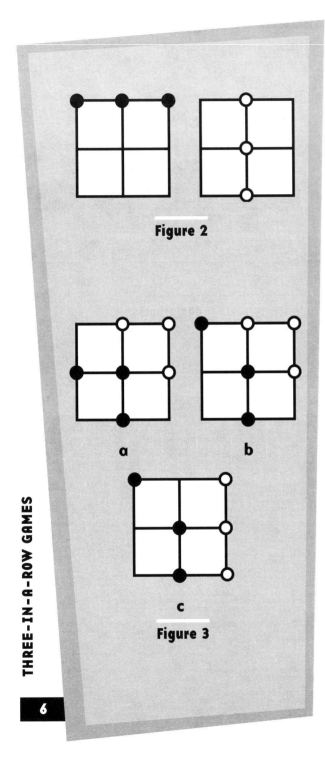

**Figure 2**

a

b

c

**Figure 3**

## PLAYING THE GAME

The game is played on the nine points where the lines intersect. The two players take turns going first. We will call the counters white and black, although they may be other colors. Player One places a white counter on any point. Then Player Two places a black counter on any point. They take turns, until each player has placed all three counters on the game board. After that, the players take turns moving their counters around on the game board. On each turn, a player moves one of his or her own counters to any empty point on the board.

Each player tries to make a row of three counters of one color, and to block the other player from making a row of three. There are six different ways to make a row: three across, and three up and down. **Figure 2**

The winner is the first player to make an unbroken row of three across or up and down. If neither player makes a row, the game is a draw. The players can decide to call the game a draw at any time. If both players are careful, a game can go on for a long time.

The players try to move their counters so that they have two different ways to make a row on their next move. This is called a trap. **Figure 3**

**a.** White has set a trap

**b.** Black can block only one row

**c.** White makes a row and wins the game

## THINGS TO THINK ABOUT

Can you find a different way to set a trap?

Where should the first player start? Is it easier for Player One to win the game than for Player Two?

## HOW NINE HOLES BECAME TIC-TAC-TOE

Imagine how the game of Nine Holes might have become Tic-Tac-Toe. It could have happened in an English schoolroom. The schoolmaster had given the students several long addition exercises to work out on their slates. While the master was calling on the children on the front bench, a boy in the back nudged the student next to him.

"Got a knife to cut lines in the bench for Nine Holes?"

"No. But we can draw the lines on my slate."

They soon had a lively game going, with pebbles and pieces of chalk as playing pieces.

Suddenly they heard the schoolmaster call out their names. Startled, they let the buttons and chalk clatter to the floor. The master gave them 10 more sums as punishment for playing games in class.

The next morning one of the boys had a wonderful idea. They could make marks on the slate instead of moving buttons and pebbles. One player could mark O's (or noughts, as they say in England) and the other could mark X's (or crosses). And the marks would go in the spaces, not on the points of the game board. As soon as the schoolmaster had turned his back, they tried out the new game on a board with nine spaces, like this. **Figure 4** Before the end of the day, the whole class was playing Noughts and Crosses. That's the name they gave Tic-Tac-Toe in England. Soon the game had spread all over England.

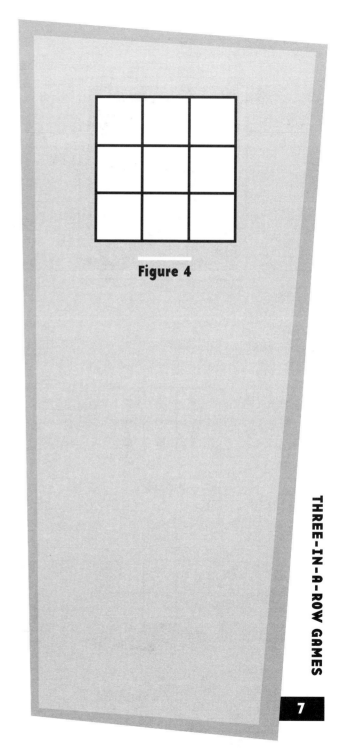

**Figure 4**

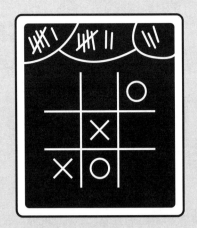

**Figure 5**

| T | I | C |
|---|---|---|
| T | A | C |
| T | O | E |

**Figure 6**

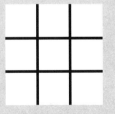

Tic-Tac-Toe diagram

**Figure 7**

# Tic-Tac-Toe

Tic-Tac-Toe, also called Noughts and Crosses in England, was a favorite game of English schoolboys. They would draw tiny game boards in the corners of their slates. When a boy was called upon to show his work, all he had to do was wet his finger and wipe away all the evidence. But it was not long before sharp-eared schoolmasters learned to recognize the click-clack of Tic-Tac-Toe games going on behind their backs!

In their free time, two children would agree at the start to play a certain number of games, usually 20. At the end of each game, they marked the score at the top of the slate—one point for the winner of each game. Then they erased the game board and drew a new one for the next game. A tied game was scored in the center space at the top of the slate. Children called it "one for Old Nick." **Figure 5**

Today Tic-Tac-Toe is the most popular three-in-a-row game in the world. **Figure 6**

Some English children, when they win, call out:

> "Tit-tat-toe,
> Here I go,
> Three jolly butcher boys
> All in a row!"

When the game ends in a draw, children in the United States may say, "It's a tie, cat's eye!"

## MATERIALS
- Sheet of paper
- Two pencils
- Ruler

## DRAWING THE GAME BOARD
Draw this diagram on a sheet of paper. **Figure 7**

## PLAYING THE GAME
**1.** Each player has a pencil. Toss a coin, or decide in some other way who will make the first move. The players should take turns going first,

because the first to go has a much better chance of winning. Player One uses the mark X. Player Two uses the mark O.

**2.** The game is played in the nine spaces set off by the lines. Player One writes X in any of the nine spaces. Then Player Two marks O in an empty space. The players take turns placing their marks in the spaces.

**3.** Each player tries to get three of his or her marks in a line—across, or up and down, or along a diagonal. This line of three marks is called a row. There are eight different ways to make a row: **Figure 8**
   **a.** Across: three ways
   **b.** Up and down: three ways
   **c.** Diagonally: two ways

**4.** The winner is the first player to get three in a row. If neither player can make a row, the game is called a draw, or a tied game.

## THINGS TO THINK ABOUT AND DO

Here are three diagrams to show the first three moves in a game. Copy the diagrams on your own sheet of paper. Play with a friend, or pretend that you are two players taking turns. Finish the game so that Player One wins with a row of three X's. **Figure 9**
   **a.** Player One marks an X
   **b.** Player Two marks an O
   **c.** Player One marks an X
Then start all over again. Copy the three diagrams, and finish the game so that it ends in a draw—nobody wins or loses.

Then start again. This time, try to finish so that Player Two is the winner with a row of three O's. It won't be easy!

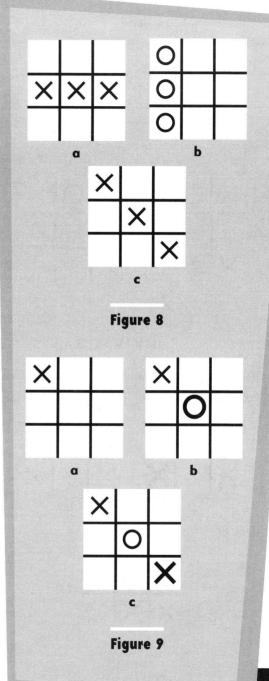

Figure 8

Figure 9

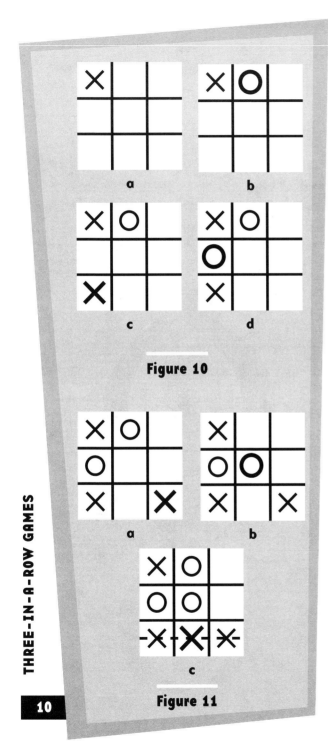

a          b

c          d

**Figure 10**

a          b

c

**Figure 11**

## HOW TO BE A GOOD PLAYER

Player One can set a trap for Player Two. Player One can plan her second move so that Player Two is forced to go in a particular space. Here is one way to do it. **Figure 10**

**a.** First move

**b.** Second move

**c.** Player One prepares to make a row

**d.** Player Two blocks that row

On the fifth move in the game Player One tries to set up two possible ways to make a row. This is a trap because Player Two can block only one of these rows. Player One is the winner. **Figure 11**

**a.** Player One sets a trap

**b.** Sixth move

**c.** Player One wins.

There are several other ways for Player One to set traps. See how many you can find.

If you go first, you probably won't lose. If you go second, you probably won't win. For Tic-Tac-Toe to be a fair game, the players should take turns going first.

## CHANGING THE RULES

After you have figured out all the good moves, Tic-Tac-Toe can be rather boring. Here are three different ways to play the game.

**1.** Rule that neither player may make the first move in the center.

**2.** Play eight-move Tic-Tac-Toe. Each player makes exactly four moves, and gets a point for each row he or she makes.

**3.** Play Toe-Tac-Tic. The first player to make a row is the loser.

# Magic Square Tic-Tac-Toe from Ancient China

Some people believe that a certain arrangement of numbers on a Tic-Tac-Toe diagram can bring good luck. Every line of three numbers has the same sum. This arrangement is called a magic square.

It is said that a Chinese emperor was the first person to see a magic square. Over 4,000 years ago a large turtle swam close to his ship. The pattern on the turtle's back was a wonderful arrangement of numbers. Every row, every column, and each diagonal added up to 15. No wonder the Chinese thought it was magic. In time, people all over the world were making magic squares. **Figure 12**

## MATERIALS
- Sheet of unlined paper, at least 7 inches (17 cm) square
- Pencil and markers
- 2 sheets of heavy paper or cardboard, at least 8 1/2 inches (22 cm) square
- Scissors
- Ruler
- Glue stick

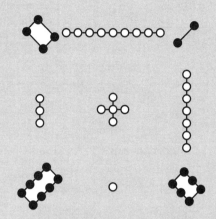

**A Chinese magic square, with knots in black and white cord showing the numbers**

**Figure 12**

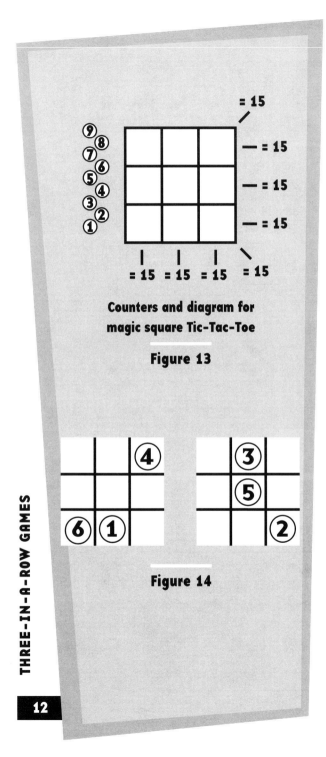

**Counters and diagram for magic square Tic-Tac-Toe**

**Figure 13**

**Figure 14**

## MAKING THE GAME BOARD AND COUNTERS

**1.** On the sheet of paper draw a 6-by-6-inch (15 cm X 15 cm) square.

**2.** Subdivide the square into nine small squares, each 2-inch (5 cm) square.

**3.** Glue the paper to the cardboard. Decorate your game board with markers or crayons.

**4.** Cut out nine small disks or squares from heavy paper and number them from one to nine. **Figure 13**

## PLAYING THE GAME

Arrange the nine counters so that each row, each column, and each diagonal has a sum of 15. You can play this game by yourself or take turns with a partner and cooperate to make a magic square. Each player may place any one of the nine counters on the game diagram.

## THINGS TO THINK ABOUT AND DO

Complete the magic squares below. Then try to arrange the counters to make other magic squares. There are eight different magic squares. **Figure 14**

# Number Tic-Tac-Toe

The object of this game is to form rows, columns, or diagonals that add up to 15.

## MATERIALS
- Sheet of unlined paper
- Pen or marker
- Ruler
- Nine counters, numbered from one to nine (see Magic Square Tic-Tac-Toe)

## DRAWING THE GAME BOARD
Draw the diagram for Tic-Tac-Toe.
**Figure 15**

## PLAYING THE GAME
**1.** Player One takes the five odd-numbered counters: 1, 3, 5, 7, and 9. Player Two takes the four even-numbered counters: 2, 4, 6, and 8.

**2.** The players take turns placing a counter on the game board. All nine counters are used. The object is to make a row of three counters that has a sum of 15. A row may contain both odd and even numbers.

**3.** A player scores one point for each row he or she completes. A player can sometimes make two or even three rows in one move.

**4.** The player with more points is the winner. **Figure 16a** and **Figure 16b**

## TAKING TURNS
For the next game, the players exchange counters.

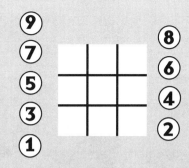

**Counters and diagram for number Tic-Tac-Toe**

**Figure 15**

a   b

a. **Player One gets ready to move**

b. **Player One has made two rows in one move, and earns two points**

**Figure 16**

# Achi from Ghana

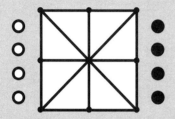

**Figure 17**

G hana, in West Africa, became an independent country in 1957. Before that year, the country was called the Gold Coast and was a colony of England. As you might guess, Europeans traded their wares for African gold along this coast. The name *Ghana* came from an ancient kingdom of that name, located farther north in Africa. It was known to the Arabs as the "land of gold." Over a thousand years ago, Ibn Hawkal, an Arab traveler to that land, described the king of Ghana as the wealthiest in the world.

Schoolchildren in Ghana play Achi. They draw the game diagram in the dirt and pick up pebbles to use as counters.

## MATERIALS
- Sheet of unlined paper, at least 8 inches (20 cm) square
- Pencil
- Ruler
- Colored markers or crayons
- Scissors
- Glue
- Piece of cardboard, at least 9 inches (22.5 cm) square
- 4 counters for each player, 4 light and 4 dark (beans, buttons, or coins)

## DRAWING THE GAME BOARD
**1.** Draw a square that measures 6 inches (15 cm) on each side.

**2.** With your pencil, draw the diagonals.

**3.** Draw lines that connect the midpoints of the opposite sides.

**4.** Use a marker or crayon to mark the nine points where the lines meet. **Figure 17**

**5.** Glue the paper to the cardboard and decorate your game board. You might want to draw the flag of Ghana and other appropriate symbols.

## PLAYING THE GAME

This game is played on the nine points where the lines intersect. Players take turns going first.

**1.** Player One places a light counter on any point. Then Player Two places a dark counter on any empty point. They take turns until all eight counters have been placed on the game board.

**2.** Then Player One moves one of her counters along a line to the next empty point. Jumping over a counter is not allowed. Player Two does the same with one of his counters. They continue this way, taking turns.

**3.** Each player tries to make a row of three counters of one color and block the other player from doing the same. A row can be made in eight different ways: three across, three down, and two along the diagonal. **Figure 18**

**4.** The winner is the first player to make a row of three. If neither player can get three in a row, the game ends in a draw—no winner or loser.

## THINGS TO THINK ABOUT

Where should Player One place the first counter in order to win? Player One can place the first counter on any one of the nine points on the board. There are really only three different ways to place the first counter: center, corner, and side. **Figure 19**

How is Achi like Tic-Tac-Toe? How is it different?

## CHANGING THE RULES

People play games similar to Achi in many parts of the world but often with different rules. Here are some other versions of the game you might want to try.

**Marelle (France).** Each player has three counters. Neither player may make the first move in the center.

**Tant Fant (India).** Each player has three counters. The game opens with each player's three counters already in position, as in the diagram. A row may not be made on the starting lines. There are just six different ways to make a row. **Figure 20**

In most versions of the game, each player has three counters. In other respects, they follow the rules for Achi. Here are the names of the game in other countries:

| Country | Game Names |
|---|---|
| Arabic-speaking countries | El-Qirqat |
| Iran | Hujura |
| Ireland | Cashian Gherra |
| Italy | Filo and Mulino |
| Spain | Tres en Raya |

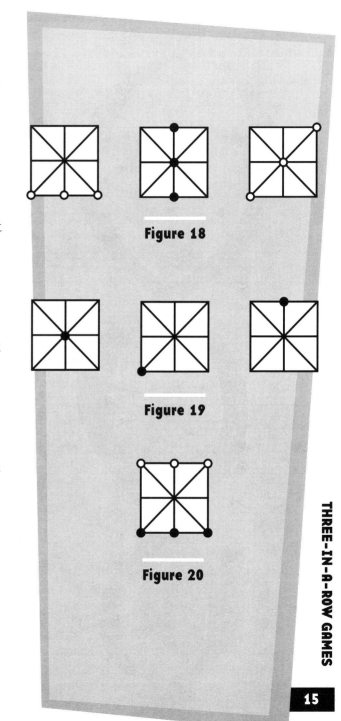

**Figure 18**

**Figure 19**

**Figure 20**

# 6 Men's Morris from Italy, France, and England

I n England, three-in-a-row games often go by the name "Morris." Long ago people played Five Men's Morris and Six Men's Morris, with five or six counters for each player. Today the most popular version is Nine Men's Morris. Six Men's Morris is a good preparation for this more popular game.

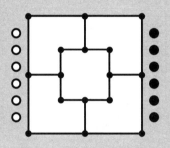

**Figure 21**

## MATERIALS
- Pencil
- Ruler
- Sheet of unlined paper, at least 8 inches (20 cm) square
- Colored markers or crayons
- Glue
- Piece of cardboard, at least 9 inches (22.5 cm) square
- 6 counters for each player, of two different types (beans, buttons, coins, or checkers)

## DRAWING THE GAME BOARD
**1.** Use the pencil and ruler to draw two squares on the paper, one inside the other. Plan carefully so that the board fits on the paper and there is enough space to move the counters.

**2.** Draw four lines connecting the midpoints of the sides, as in the diagram. **Figure 21**

**3.** Go over the pencil lines with markers or crayons. Mark the 16 points where the lines intersect.

**4.** Glue the paper to the cardboard. Decorate your game board with markers or crayons.

## PLAYING THE GAME

**1.** The two players take turns placing one counter at a time on an empty point on the game board.

**2.** When all 12 counters have been placed, the players take turns moving one counter at a time along a line to the next empty point. Jumping over a counter is not allowed.

**3.** Each player tries to make a row of three counters of the same kind along any straight line. A row of three is called a "mill." There are eight different ways to make a mill.

**4.** A player who makes a mill at any stage of the game is allowed to remove one of the other player's counters from the board. However, a counter may not be removed from the opponent's mill unless no other counter of that color is on the game board. Captured counters are not used again in that game.

**5.** The loser is the player who has only two counters left on the board, or is blocked from moving.

## HOW TO BE A GOOD PLAYER

Whenever possible, place your counters so that they can move in two or three directions. The black counter can move in any one of three ways. The white counter can move in only two different ways. **Figure 22**

Place three counters so that you can shift one back and forth to open and close a mill. Every time you close a mill, you capture one of your opponent's counters. **Figure 23**

## THINGS TO THINK ABOUT

Can all 12 counters be placed on the board without forming a mill?

Can you think of a plan that allows you to open and close a mill many times?

## CHANGING THE RULES

Play Five Men's Morris. In this game, each player has five counters. Follow all the other rules for Six Men's Morris.

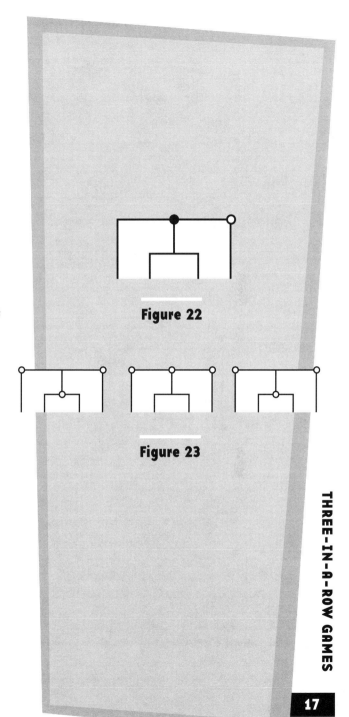

**Figure 22**

**Figure 23**

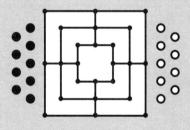

**Figure 24**

# Alquerque de Nueve from Spain

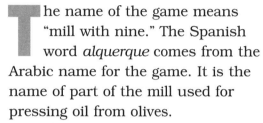

The name of the game means "mill with nine." The Spanish word *alquerque* comes from the Arabic name for the game. It is the name of part of the mill used for pressing oil from olives.

In the eighth century, Arabic-speaking people from North Africa came to Spain. They taught the Spanish people games from other parts of the world, like chess and Alquerque. In the thirteenth century the Spanish king Alfonso the Wise had this information written down in the *Book of Games*, the first game book to appear in Europe.

Three-in-a-row games were becoming popular among rich and poor all over Europe. Wealthy homes and royal courts had beautiful game boards and game tables. Some of these treasures are now displayed in museums.

A thousand years ago, sailors carved a game board on the wooden deck of a Viking ship. This ship, the burial place of a Viking prince, was dug up in Gokstad, Norway, and is in a museum. A book by the Italian writer Petrarch shows a game between two apes!

Shepherds would dig lines in the earth to make game boards that were sometimes as large as a room. In his play *A Midsummer Night's Dream*, William Shakespeare described the effects of a rainstorm:

**The Nine Men's Morris is filled up with mud.**

Boys would carve game diagrams on bins and stable floors. They played whenever they had a few minutes to spare from their work. Young men waiting for their carriages might chalk the lines on the flat top of a tall hat and play a quick game with pennies.

The game is known by many different names, but the rules are the same. See the end of this activity for the names of the game in various countries.

## MATERIALS

See Six Men's Morris (page 16). Each player has nine counters.

## DRAWING THE GAME BOARD

**1.** Use the pencil and ruler to draw three squares on the paper, one inside the other. Measure carefully, so that the board fits on the paper and there is enough room to move the counters.

**2.** Draw four lines connecting the midpoints of the sides, as in the diagram. **Figure 24**

**3.** Go over the pencil lines with markers or crayons. Mark the 24 points where the lines intersect.

**4.** Then glue the paper to the cardboard. Decorate your game board with markers or crayons.

## PLAYING THE GAME

The rules for Alquerque de Nueve, called Nine Men's Morris in England, are similar to those for Six Men's Morris, page 17. The main differences are:

**1.** Each player has nine counters.

**2.** The game is played on the 24 points where the lines intersect.

**3.** There are 16 different ways to make a mill, or three-in-a-row. A mill can be made on the line connecting the midpoints of the sides of the three squares. **Figure 25**

## HOW TO BE A GOOD PLAYER

**1.** Follow the hints for Six Men's Morris (page 17).

**2.** Try to form a "cross mill." In the diagram, the lines connecting the four counters form a cross. White can make a mill by moving any one of the four counters into the center of the cross. **Figure 26**

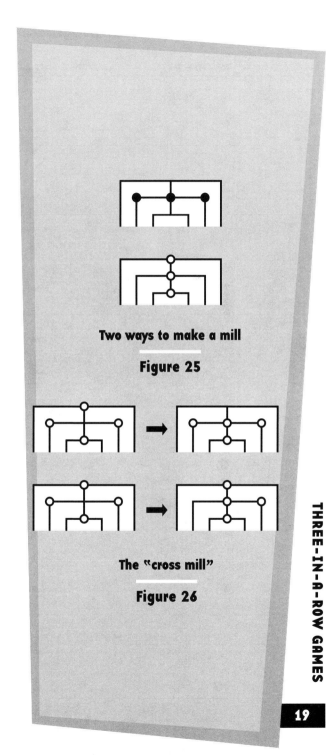

**Two ways to make a mill**

**Figure 25**

**The "cross mill"**

**Figure 26**

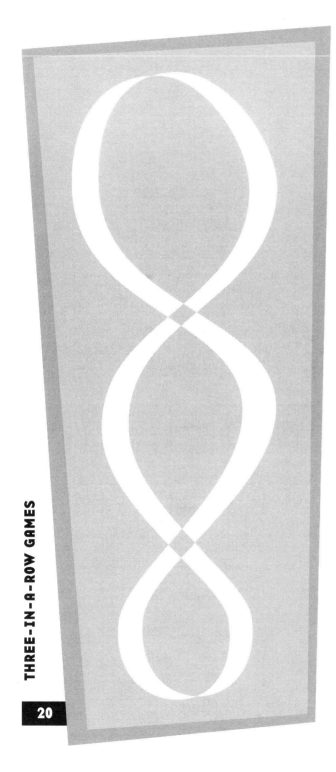

## CHANGING THE RULES

Play with dice, as described in the Spanish *Book of Games*. During the "placing" stage, the players take turns using three dice. If the outcome is any of these combinations:

6–5–4     6–3–3     5–2–2     4–1–1

the player captures a counter from the other player, and also places his or her own counter on the board. If this player can also make a mill, he or she can remove two of the opponent's counters from the board. If any other combination of numbers turns up on the dice, the play continues by the usual rules.

## THE NAME OF THE GAME AROUND THE WORLD

This version of the game is one of the most popular in the world. In many European countries, the name includes the word for "mill."

| Country | Game Name |
|---|---|
| Arabic-speaking countries | Dris |
| England | Nine Men's Morris |
| Germany | Muhle |
| Greece | Triodi |
| Hungary | Malom |
| India | Nao-guti |
| Italy | Mulinello |
| Native Americans of California | Yakamaido |
| Native Americans of Southwest United States | Pitarilla, Picaria, and Paitariya |
| Nigeria | Akidada |
| Norway | Molle |
| Russia | Melnitsa |
| Sweden | Qvarn |

# Jirig from Mongolia

The people of Mongolia, a land in Asia, have been herders of animals for centuries. They raise sheep, goats, horses, cows, yaks, and camels. The whole family cares for the animals and moves from place to place to find food for them.

Games and sports are important in the life of the Mongolian people. They are famous for horse racing, a summer sport. In early spring, at the time of their New Year celebration, people play board games and dominoes as part of the festivities. In the past, people believed that playing board games in summer and autumn would bring thunderstorms and wolves to attack the herds. Perhaps the real reason for banning such games was that they would take attention away from the care of the herds.

## MATERIALS
- Sheet of unlined paper, at least 8 inches (20 cm) square
- Ruler
- Pencil
- Colored markers or crayons
- Glue
- Piece of cardboard or construction paper, at least 9 inches (22.5 cm) square
- 11 counters for each player or team, two different kinds (beans, buttons, coins, or checkers)

## DRAWING THE GAME BOARD
See the directions for drawing the game board for Alquerque de Nueve (page 19). Then connect the corners of the three squares by drawing diagonal lines. Mark the 24 points where the lines intersect. **Figure 27**

## PLAYING THE GAME
The object of the game is to get a row of three counters. The row can be made along the side of a square, along a line joining the midpoints of the sides of the squares, or along a

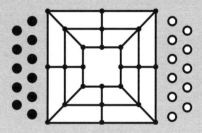

**Game board for Jirig**

**Figure 27**

diagonal line joining the corners. There are 20 ways to make a row.
**Figure 28**

**1.** The players take turns placing one counter at a time on an empty point on the board. After all the counters have been placed, the players take turns moving one marker along a line to the next empty point. Jumping over a counter is not allowed.

**2.** When a player forms a row of three, he or she removes one of the opponent's counters from the board. That counter is not used for the rest of the game. However, counters that are part of a row of three may not be removed.

**3.** The loser is the player who has only two counters on the board remaining, or is blocked from moving.

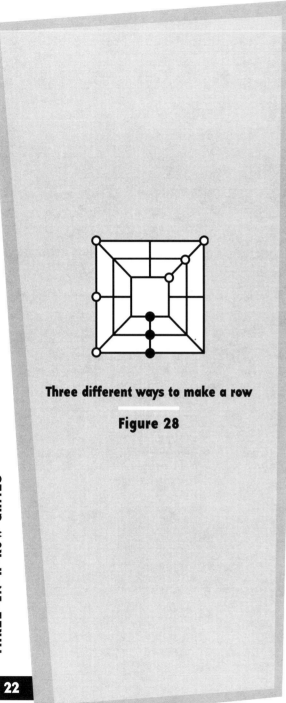

**Three different ways to make a row**

**Figure 28**

### HOW TO BE A GOOD PLAYER

See the hints for Six Men's Morris and Alquerque de Nueve.

### CHANGING THE RULES

**Play Nerenchi.** Girls and women in Sri Lanka enjoy the game called Nerenchi. The board is the same as for Jirig. Each player or team has 12 counters. A player who makes a row of three during the "placing" stage takes an extra turn and may do so for each row made. The "placing" stage ends when 22 counters are on the board. One player may have 12 counters on the board, while the other has only 10.

In the following games, each player starts with 12 counters, as in Nerenchi. The game board is the same.

| Country | Name of Game |
| --- | --- |
| China | Sam K'i |
| Korea | Kon-tjil |
| Malaysia | Dig Dig |
| Somalia | Shah and Shax |
| New England colonies (in early U.S. history) | Twelve Men's Morris |

# Murabaraba from Lesotho & South Africa

Until recently, boys in the south-ern African country of Lesotho were expected to spend their days caring for large herds of cattle. But, at the risk of punishment, they managed to get in a game of Murabaraba now and then.

Nowadays most children in Lesotho go to school during the day. Some teachers encourage their students to play Murabaraba. A recent study showed that children who knew the game did better in their school geometry lessons than those who had never played it.

Murabaraba is no longer just a boys' pastime. Girls play, too. Often two teams play against each other, while friends gather around and shout advice. The game is so popular that the game board is often marked on a large flat stone in the village square, ready for use at any time.

## MATERIALS

See the list of materials for Jirig on page 21. Each player has 12 counters.

## DRAWING THE GAME BOARD

**1.** Use the pencil and ruler to draw three squares on the sheet of paper, one inside the other. Plan your lay-out carefully so that you have enough space to move the counters.

**2.** Draw two lines connecting the midpoints of the sides of the squares. These two lines intersect in the center.

**3.** Draw four lines to connect the corners of the two larger squares. **Figure 29**

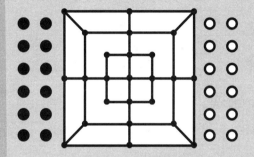

**Board for Murabaraba**

**Figure 29**

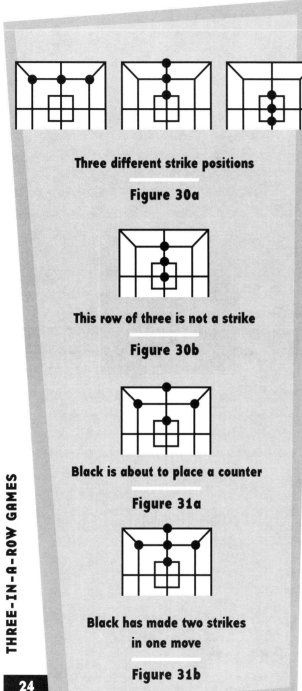

**Three different strike positions**

**Figure 30a**

**This row of three is not a strike**

**Figure 30b**

**Black is about to place a counter**

**Figure 31a**

**Black has made two strikes in one move**

**Figure 31b**

**4.** Go over the lines with markers or crayons and mark the 25 points where the lines intersect.

**5.** Glue the sheet of paper to the cardboard. If you already have a board for Alquerque de Nueve (page 19), all you need to do is connect the lines joining the midpoints of the squares, and connect the corners of the two larger squares.

## PLAYING THE GAME

The two players (or teams) take turns placing one counter at a time on an empty point on the board. This part of the game ends when all 24 counters have been placed.

**1.** The players (or teams) take turns moving one counter at a time along any line to the next empty point. Jumping over a counter is not allowed.

**2.** Each player tries to make a row of three counters of the same color. This is called a strike. But a line of three that ends in the center of the board is *not* a strike. **Figure 30a** and **Figure 30b**

**3.** A player who makes a strike may remove one of the opponent's counters from any position on the board. Captured counters are no longer used in that game.

**4.** During the "placing" stage of the game, it is possible to make two strikes at one time. When that happens, the player may capture two of the opponent's counters. **Figure 31a** and **Figure 31b**

Traps: During the "placing" stage of the game, a player who has two counters in a row must complete the strike on the next move, if possible. This situation is called a trap. If the player can, but does not, complete his or her strike on the next turn, the opponent may remove any two of this player's counters from the board.

During the "moving" stage of the game, there are no traps. If a player's counters are blocked so that none of them may move, that player either skips a turn or gives up the game.

Finish: The loser is the player who has only two counters left on the board or who is blocked and gives up. A player who has only three counters on the board may "hop" them to any empty point on the board. But usually the other player has given up or lost long before this stage.

## HOW TO BE A GOOD PLAYER

The hints and strategies for Alquerque de Nueve (page 19) are just as useful for Murabaraba.

## SAMPLE GAME

Set up your Murabaraba game board as shown in the diagram, and continue the game to the finish. All 24 counters have been placed on the board, and neither player has made a strike or been trapped. **Figure 32**

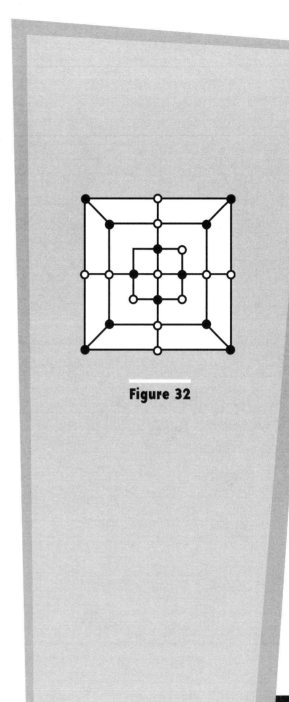

**Figure 32**

**Boards for Jirig**

**Figure 33**

# The Shape of the Game Board

The Mongolians call their three-in-a-row games Jirig. On page 21 there is an illustration of the set of squares on which they play the game. But they also play Jirig on boards having other shapes: triangles, pentagons (five-sided), and hexagons (six-sided). **Figure 33**

The rules are the same for all these game boards. The only difference is the number of counters for each player.

## THINGS TO THINK ABOUT

How many counters should each player use for the triangular board? For the pentagonal board? For the hexagonal board? To answer that question, let's look at the square board setup.

The square board has 24 points on which the game is played. Each player has 11 counters, a total of 22 counters. Suppose each player had 12 counters. Would they be able to play the game? Suppose one player had 12 and the other had 10 or 11 counters. Would that be fair? What is the largest number of counters that each player should use?

Let's look at the triangular board. How many points of intersection are there? Instead of counting every point, find a shortcut. How many points of intersection in one triangle? How many triangles? How many points total? How many counters should each player use?

Now figure out the largest number of counters for each player on the pentagonal board and on the hexagonal board. What numbers did you get in each case? (After you have figured it out, see page 153 to check your answers.)

You may have decided that the total number is two less than the number of points of intersection on the game board. That's a logical answer.

You might wonder about games like Twelve Men's Morris and others listed on page 22. Each player has 12 counters and they play on 24 points. At least one counter must be captured in the "placing" stage of the game so that the game can continue.

But what about a game like Nerenchi (page 22)? The game board has 24 points, and each player starts with 12 counters. Check to find out how that problem is solved.

Each game board we have discussed here has an even number of points. But in Zimbabwe, a country in southern Africa, people play on a board with an odd number of points. The game is called *Tsoro Yematatu,* the "stone game played with three." The board has seven points, and each player has three counters. **Figure 34**

Another game with an odd number of points is Murabaraba (page 23), also popular in southern Africa. If all 24 counters are placed on the game board, only one empty point remains. The sample game on page 25 is a good example. Have you tried to finish the game? That is a real challenge!

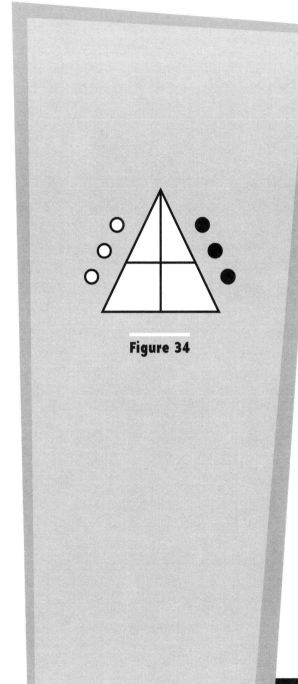

**Figure 34**

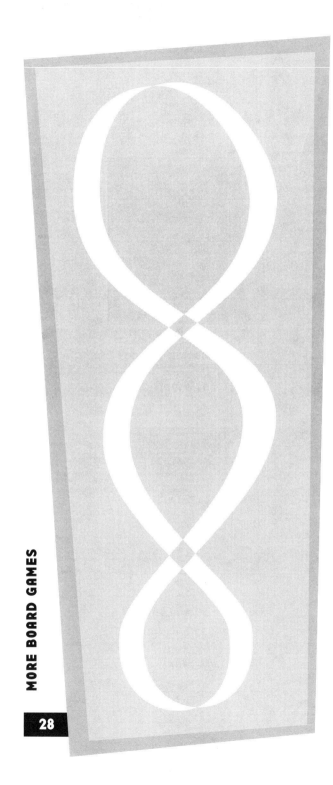

# More Board Games

In this chapter you will learn about two major types of games, all of which are for two players. The first two games are from lands in Asia. In both games, tigers threaten to capture and eat smaller animals. In the first game, leopards are in danger and must defend themselves against just one tiger. In the second game, the three tigers are about to pounce upon some of the 15 lambs. Which animals are stronger, the tigers or the other animals? Did you know that tigers live in Asia, but not in Africa?

The next four games are called Mankala games. *Mankala* is an Arabic word that means "transferring." Counters are transferred from one cup to another on a game board. Mankala is thousands of years old, and is played in most African countries, as well as in the Philippines, Sri Lanka, Central Asia, and Arabic-speaking countries. Africans captured in the slave trade brought the game to parts of the Americas—eastern Brazil, Suriname,

Guyana, and the Caribbean Islands—where it is still popular today. In recent years Mankala games were introduced into the United States. In the past, slaveholders in the United States, in an effort to increase control over their slaves, removed all traces of African culture and did not allow their slaves to play the game.

You can learn about the culture of the people who play by noticing the names they give to the game. In Sudan, a country in northeast Africa, people are herders of animals, and the name of the game refers to goats and cows. They often dig out holes in the sand to create a makeshift game board. On the other hand, players in Ghana, once a wealthy kingdom, buy houses and place their captured loot in the treasury. They sometimes play on beautifully carved game boards that have been in the family for generations.

Look on a map for the countries mentioned in this chapter and learn more about them.

# Leopards and Tigers from Thailand

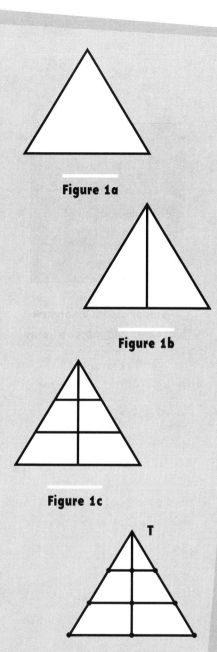

**Figure 1a**

**Figure 1b**

**Figure 1c**

Game board

**Figure 1d**

This is a simple form of a "leop-ard" game that is popular in southern Asia. In this game for two players, called *Hat Diviyan Keliya* in the language of Thailand, one player has just one playing piece, called the Tiger. The other player has six counters, called Leopards. Can you imagine why the counters have the names of these animals?

Find Thailand on the map. It used to be called Siam.

## MATERIALS

- Sheet of unlined paper, about 11 inches (27.5 cm) long
- Piece of cardboard, about 12 inches (30 cm) long
- Ruler
- Pencil
- Pen or marker
- Glue
- 6 counters of one kind, 1 counter of another kind (beans, buttons, checkers, or coins)

## DRAWING THE GAME BOARD

**1.** The game board is in the shape of an isosceles triangle (it has two equal sides). With a pencil and ruler, draw the triangle as shown in the diagram. **Figure 1a**

**2.** Draw an altitude that divides the triangle in half. **Figure 1b**

**3.** Draw two lines parallel to the base of the triangle, as in the diagram. **Figure 1c**

**4.** Go over the lines with a pen or marker. Mark the 10 intersection points on which the game is played. **Figure 1d**

**5.** Glue the paper to the cardboard. You may want to decorate the game board and keep it to use again.

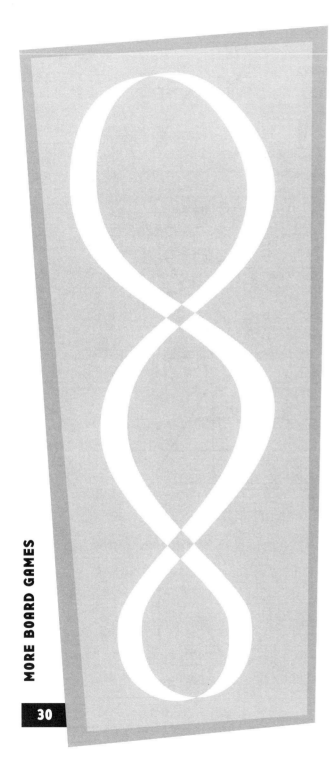

## PLAYING THE GAME

**1.** Player One has one counter called the Tiger. Player Two has six counters called Leopards.

**2.** Players move from point to point on the game board. Player One moves first, and places the Tiger at the top point *T* (apex) of the triangle. Player Two places one Leopard on any empty point. The players take turns. The Tiger moves along a line to the next empty point, while Player Two places all the Leopards, one at a time, on empty points. The Leopards may not change their positions until all the Leopards have been placed on the board.

**3.** Continue taking turns, moving one counter at a time along a line to the next empty point. Only the Tiger may capture Leopards. The Tiger captures by jumping over a Leopard along a line to the next point, if it is empty (just like in checkers). The Tiger then captures that Leopard. The Tiger may be able to capture more than one Leopard in one move if the point along the same line just beyond the Leopard is free. Meanwhile the Leopards try to block the Tiger so that it cannot move.

**4.** The Leopards win if the Tiger can no longer move. The Tiger wins if it captures so many Leopards that the Tiger can no longer be blocked.

## THINGS TO THINK ABOUT

Would it be wise to place the first Leopard directly under the Tiger?

Where is the safest place to put the first Leopard?

## CHANGING THE RULES

Children in Sri Lanka play with one Tiger and seven Leopards. Otherwise the rules are the same.

Find Sri Lanka on the map. It used to be a British colony and was called Ceylon. In 1948 it became an independent country. In 1972 the country adopted its traditional name, Sri Lanka, which means "resplendent island."

# Lambs and Tigers from India

This game for two players is also called Pulijudam. It is a more complicated version of Leopards and Tigers (page 29). It is played in India and neighboring countries.

Player One has three counters, called the Tigers. Player Two has fifteen counters, called the Lambs. Can you guess which type of animal is likely to capture the other type?

## MATERIALS

The same as for Leopards and Tigers (page 29), except that Player One has three counters of one type and Player Two has fifteen counters of a different type

## DRAWING THE GAME BOARD

**1.** Use your pencil and ruler to draw a tall narrow triangle. **Figure 2a**

**2.** Draw another triangle with the same apex (top), and wider than the first triangle. **Figure 2b**

**3.** Draw a trapezoid (four-sided figure) intersecting the triangles. **Figure 2c**

**4.** Go over the lines with a pen or marker.

**5.** Mark the 17 points where lines intersect. The game is played on these points. Three points near the top are marked with the letter *T*. **Figure 2d**

## PLAYING THE GAME

**1.** Player One moves first and places one Tiger in one of the points marked *T*. Then Player Two places a Lamb on any point not marked *T*.

**2.** The players take turns. Player One must first place the Tigers in the three marked points before they can be moved. Player Two must place all 15 Lambs before they can be moved.

**3.** The players continue to take turns, moving one counter at a time along a line to the next empty point.

Triangle

Figure 2a

Draw another triangle

Figure 2b

Draw a trapezoid

Figure 2c

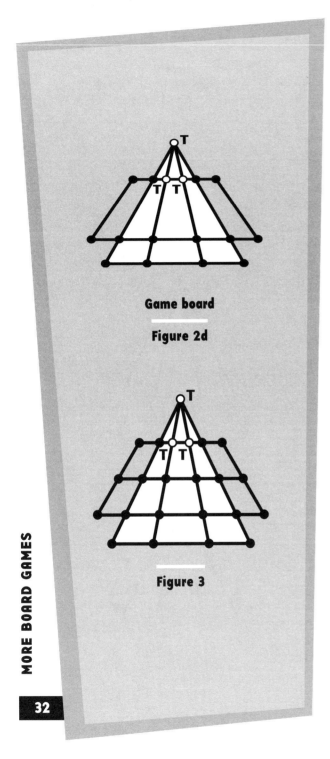

**Game board**

**Figure 2d**

**Figure 3**

Only a Tiger may capture, by jumping over a Lamb along a line to the next point, provided it is empty. This Lamb is then removed from the game. The Tiger may be able to capture more than one Lamb in one move. Meanwhile the Lambs try to block the Tigers so that they cannot move.

**4.** The Lambs win if they block the three Tigers. The Tigers win when so few Lambs are left on the board that they cannot block the Tigers.

## THINGS TO THINK ABOUT

There are 17 points on the board, but 18 counters in the game. What must happen so that the game can continue?

## CHANGING THE RULES

Try the same game on a larger game board. Draw a line connecting the midpoints of the two sides of the trapezoid. Mark the six new points. Now the board has 23 points. **Figure 3**

# Tchuka Ruma from Indonesia

**H**ere is a game you can play by yourself. You will move the counters a few at a time until they all land in one place, called the Ruma. It is a good introduction to the Mankala games, also called "games of transferring," that you will find later in this chapter. Indonesian children often dig holes in the sand and pick up pebbles or sticks to use as counters. You may play on a paper "board."

Find Indonesia on a map of Asia. The country sits on the Equator and consists of 17,000 islands. People live on about 6,000 of these islands.

## MATERIALS
- Sheet of paper about 11 inches (27.5 cm) long
- Sheet of cardboard, 11 or 12 inches (30 cm) long
- Pencil
- Ruler
- Pen or markers
- Glue

- 8 counters (buttons, beans, coins, or checkers)

## DRAWING THE GAME BOARD

**1.** Draw a rectangle measuring 10 inches by 2 inches (25 cm by 5 cm).

**2.** On each long side, make a mark every 2 inches (5 cm). **Figure 4a**

**3.** Connect the marks. The rectangle is divided into 5 small squares.

**4.** Go over the lines with a pen or marker. Write "Ruma" in the last square on the right. **Figure 4b**

**5.** Glue the paper to the cardboard. Decorate the game board if you like.

## PLAYING THE GAME

**1.** To start, place two counters in each small square. Moves are made from left to right. **Figure 4c**

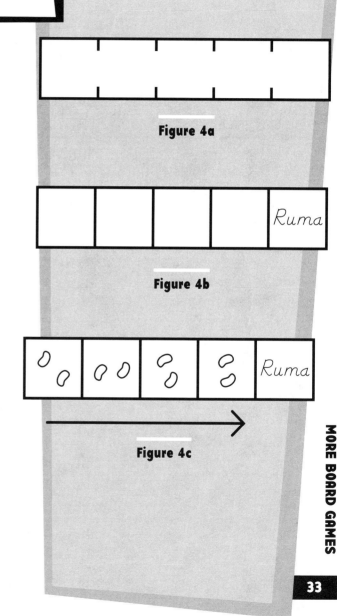

**Figure 4a**

**Figure 4b**

**Figure 4c**

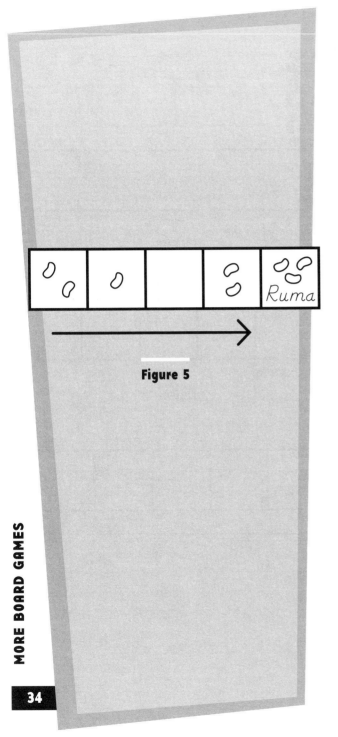

**Figure 5**

**2.** Pick up the counters from any square and drop them, one in each square, in the next few squares, including the Ruma. This is called sowing the seeds. If you drop a counter in the Ruma and you still have one or more counters in your hand, go back to the first square and continue sowing. Plan your move so that the last counter does not fall into an empty square.

**3.** After you have dropped the last seed, pick up all the seeds in that square and continue sowing as before. If the last seed falls into the Ruma, you may pick up the seeds from any square and sow them. But if the last seed in your hand falls into a square that was empty, you lose the game. You win when all eight seeds are in the Ruma.

## THINGS TO THINK ABOUT

Here is a hint about what to watch out for. Set up your board so that it looks like the diagram. You have two seeds in the first square, one seed in the second square, none in the third square, and two in the fourth square. The Ruma has three seeds. Show that you will lose the game, no matter which square you start from.
**Figure 5**

## CHANGING THE RULES

Make a longer board that has five squares and a Ruma. You will need 10 counters. Otherwise the rules are the same as above.

# Little Goat Game from Sudan

This is a game of transfer for two players. It is called *Um el Tuweisat* in northern Sudan, a country in northeast Africa. It is an easy version of the Cow Game (see page 37). Children dig holes in the sand and gather seeds to use as counters. Playing this game on a flat sheet of paper helps you to see exactly what happens with each move.

## MAKING THE GAME BOARD
- Sheet of heavy paper or card-board
- Ruler
- Pencil
- Marker
- 2 small bowls or cups
- 12 counters of one kind (buttons, beans, pebbles, or shells)

## DRAWING THE GAME BOARD
**1.** Draw a rectangle measuring 6 inches by 4 inches (15 cm by 10 cm).

**2.** Divide the rectangle into six small squares measuring 2 inches by 2 inches (5 cm by 5 cm).

**3.** Go over the lines with a marker.

**4.** Place one bowl or cup, called the storage bowl, at each end of the game board. **Figure 6**

## PLAYING THE GAME
**1.** The players sit facing each other with the game board between them. Place two beans or other counters in each square. The three squares, called cups, on each side of the board belong to the player nearest them. The storage bowl to the right of each player belongs to that player. **Figure 7**

**2.** To move, Player One picks up the beans in any one of her cups and drops one bean into each cup. This is called sowing the seeds. The arrow shows in which direction the move is made. **Figure 8**

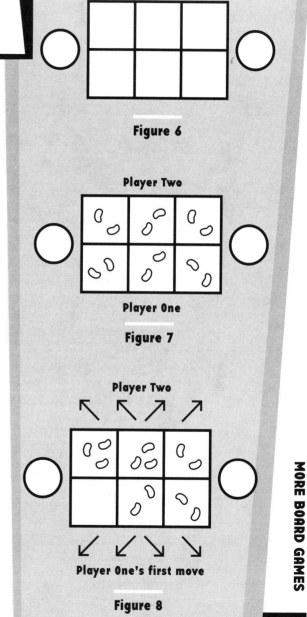

**Figure 6**

Player Two

Player One

**Figure 7**

Player Two

Player One's first move

**Figure 8**

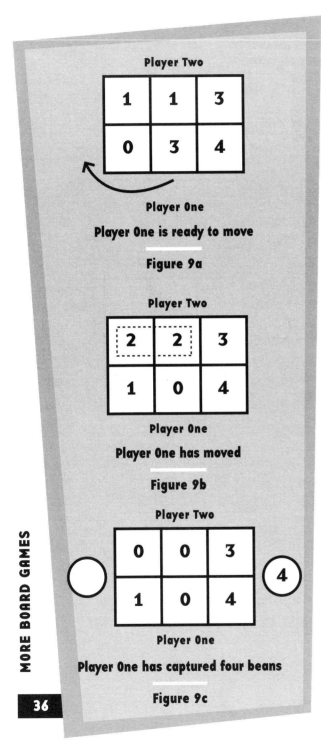

**Player Two**

| 1 | 1 | 3 |
|---|---|---|
| 0 | 3 | 4 |

**Player One**

**Player One is ready to move**

**Figure 9a**

**Player Two**

| 2 | 2 | 3 |
|---|---|---|
| 1 | 0 | 4 |

**Player One**

**Player One has moved**

**Figure 9b**

**Player Two**

| 0 | 0 | 3 |
|---|---|---|
| 1 | 0 | 4 |

**Player One**

**Player One has captured four beans**

**Figure 9c**

A move from the right-hand cup goes to the right and around the corner to Player Two's side. A move from the left-hand cup goes to the left and around the corner to the opposite side. A move from the center cup can go in either direction.

**3.** Then Player Two picks up all the beans in any one of his cups. He drops one bean in each cup in the direction shown by the arrow. The players take turns in this way. Do not sow beans into the storage bowls.

**4.** Captures are made from the opponent's side of the board. If the last bean in any move makes a group of two in a cup on the opponent's side, the player captures these two beans and places them into her storage bowl. Then, going backward, if the cup just before the captured beans also has two beans, the player may capture them and place them in her bowl. Continue to capture as long as each cup has just two beans and is on the far side of the board.

Suppose that the board is set up as in **Figure 9a**. Player One is ready to move. She can capture four beans and place them in her bowl. **Figure 9b and Figure 9c**

**5.** The game ends when one person has no beans left on his or her side of the board. The other player puts the remaining beans in his or her bowl. Then the beans in the storage bowls are counted. The player who has captured more beans is the winner.

### THINGS TO THINK ABOUT AND DO
Practice playing this game by yourself to learn how to make good moves. Practice different kinds of moves and see how many beans you can capture.

### CHANGING THE RULES
Sudanese children start the game with three beans in each cup. They capture by twos.

# Cow Game from Sudan

O nce you have practiced the Little Goat Game (page 35), try this more challenging version. People in Sudan call the game *Um el Bagara*. Another name is *Mangala*. This name is similar to *Mankala*, the Arabic word for "transferring." Mankala games are popular in most of Africa and in several other parts of the world. The game is for two players.

## MATERIALS

- Empty (one dozen) egg carton, with the lid removed
- Colored markers
- 2 small bowls or cups
- 50 counters of one kind (beans, buttons, pebbles, or shells)

## MAKING THE GAME BOARD

The board for this game has five cups on each side, ten cups altogether. You may remove the two cups at the end of the egg carton, or just ignore the two end cups. You might want to decorate the carton with African patterns and colors. Place one bowl at each end of the board as a storage bowl to hold the captured beans. **Figure 10a**

## PLAYING THE GAME

**1.** The players sit facing each other with the game board between them. Place five beans or other counters in each cup. The five cups on each side of the board belong to the player nearest them. The storage bowl to the right of each player belongs to that player.

**2.** To move, players take turns picking up all the beans in any one of their cups and dropping them, one bean in each cup, starting with the cup next to the starting cup. This is called "sowing the seeds."

Notice the arrows in the diagram of the board. These arrows tell you which direction your move takes.

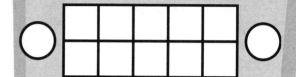

**Figure 10a**

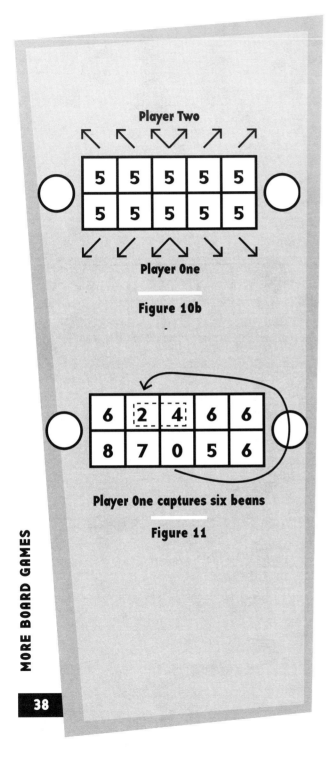

**Player Two**

| 5 | 5 | 5 | 5 | 5 |
|---|---|---|---|---|
| 5 | 5 | 5 | 5 | 5 |

**Player One**

**Figure 10b**

| 6 | 2 | 4 | 6 | 6 |
|---|---|---|---|---|
| 8 | 7 | 0 | 5 | 6 |

**Player One captures six beans**

**Figure 11**

Moves from the player's two right-hand cups go to the right. Moves from the two left-hand cups go to the left. Moves from the center cup can go either right or left. Some beans will fall into the cups on the other player's side of the board. Do not "sow" into the storage bowls. **Figure 10b**

**3.** If the last bean of a move lands in one of the opponent's cups and makes a two or a four, these beans are captured and placed in the player's storage bowl. If the cup just before this one also contains two or four beans, those beans may be captured as well. The same is true for the cup just before that one, and so on, as long as each cup contains two or four beans and lies on the opponent's side of the board. **Figure 11** shows that Player One has sowed six beans from her center cup, and captured six beans from her opponent's cups.

A move cannot begin from a cup containing just one bean.

If a player cannot make a move, he or she must skip that turn, and continue skipping until a legal move is possible.

**4.** When neither player can move, the game is over. Each player may capture the beans on his or her side of the board and add them to the storage bowls. The player who has captured the larger number of beans is the winner.

### THINGS TO THINK ABOUT AND DO

Play both sides by yourself. You may want to start with three beans in each cup, or 30 beans altogether. It will be a real challenge to remember the direction of each move! Plan the best moves that will lead to capturing the opponent's beans.

There are many versions of the Mankala game. In some versions, moves are made in only one direction, either to the right or to the left. You may want to change some of the rules and perhaps invent a new game.

# Adi from Ghana

hana is a country in West Africa. You may have played the Achi game from Ghana, described on page 14. The children of Ghana play several different versions of Mankala, the "game of transferring." The most popular version in the United States is called Oware (Oh-WAHR-ee), played by the Asante people of central Ghana. In southern Ghana people are more likely to play Adi (Ah-dee). Both games are played on a board that has two rows of six cups each, with four counters in each cup at the start of the game, but the rules are different.

The cups are called houses. Children gather Adi seeds from the Aditi bushes and place four seeds in each of the houses. At each end of the board is a storage cup called the treasury. The object of the game is to buy up all the opponent's houses.

## MATERIALS
- Empty (one dozen) egg carton with the lid removed
- Colored markers
- 2 small bowls or cups
- 48 counters of one kind (beans, buttons, pebbles, or shells)

## MAKING THE GAME BOARD
The board has six cups on each side, twelve cups total. An egg carton makes a perfect game board. You might want to decorate it with patterns that are popular in Ghana or other African countries. Place one bowl or cup at each end of the board as the treasury to hold the captured seeds. **Figure 12**

## PLAYING THE GAME
**1.** The players sit facing each other with the game board between them. They place four seeds in each space. The six spaces, called houses, on each side of the board belong to the

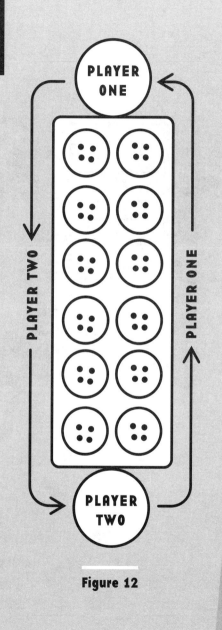

**Figure 12**

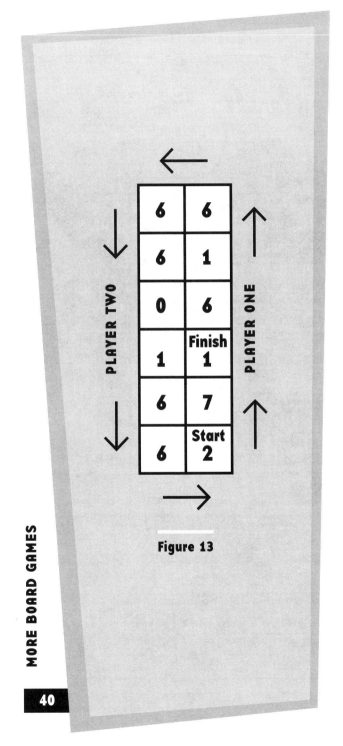

**Figure 13**

player nearest them. The treasury to the right of each player belongs to that player.

**2.** To move, Player One picks up the four seeds from any house on her side of the board and drops them, one by one, into each house, going around to the right, leaving the starting house empty. Some seeds may fall into the houses on the opponent's side of the board. Do not drop seeds into the treasury.

**3.** This game is played in laps. If the last seed falls into a house already containing seeds, the player picks them all up and continues around, each time picking up all the seeds from the house in which she has just dropped her last seed. Her turn ends when the last seed falls into an empty house. Then Player Two does the same thing, starting on his side of the board.

One move may cover a lot of ground. Suppose that Player One makes the first move from the first house on her side. The diagram

shows the game board at the end of her move. She has gone around the whole board more than twice, and dropped her last seed in the third house on her side. Carry out this move and see whether your board looks like the one in the diagram.
**Figure 13**

**4.** If a player makes a house of four as he drops his last seed, he captures that group of seeds, whether they lie on his side or the opponent's side of the board. He may also capture any house of four that appears on his side of the board, even if it happens during his opponent's turn. He must be quick enough to pick up the four seeds before the opponent drops a fifth seed into that house. He places the captured seeds in his treasury.

If a player has no seeds on her side when it is her turn, she skips her turn.

**5.** When there are eight seeds left on the board, the player who captures the next four also gets the last four. That ends the first round of the game.

**6.** The winner of the round is the player with more than enough seeds in her treasury to fill her houses with four in each. She uses the left-over seeds to "buy" any empty houses she chooses from her opponent by filling them with her own seeds.

**7.** The players then start the next round. Suppose Player One has bought eight houses, the six on her side and any two she chooses on the other side. In the next round she owns all eight houses and fills them with her 32 seeds. Her opponent may use only four houses. The rules are the same as for the first round.

The object of the game is to buy all the opponent's houses and own the whole board.

## THINGS TO THINK ABOUT AND DO

**1.** When you are learning the game, you may want to place three seeds in each house. How will you change the other rules? You may decide that captures are made in groups of three.

**2.** Another way to simplify the game is to use a board having four houses in each row.

**3.** Play both sides by yourself to see how the game works out.

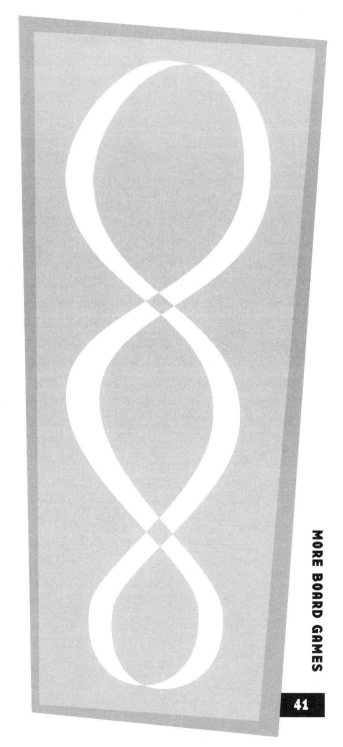

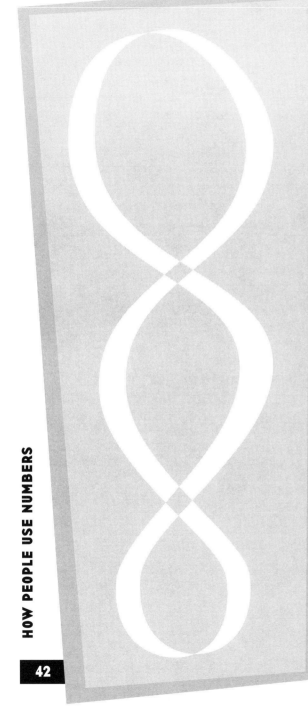

# 3

# How People Use Numbers

The activities in this chapter tell you how people have used numbers in many societies, ancient and modern, including our own.

It starts with the abacus. You may have seen, or even used, an abacus. Little children play with them as toys, but they have been used for calculating for hundreds of years. You will learn how to make your own Russian abacus and Chinese abacus. They are not the same.

People in all societies need some way to keep track of time. Of course you are familiar with the 12-month calendar. There have been other types of calendars, some based on the cycles of the moon, others depending on the rotation of the earth around the sun. You will also read about the Chinese zodiac and learn what is meant by "The Year of the Rat."

We use metal coins and paper bills as money. In other societies, shells, beads, and cocoa beans have served this purpose. Imagine breaking a silver coin into eight pieces, or "bits," for small change!

The chapter ends with ways to save. You can learn how to save cans, how to save energy, and even how to save children's lives!

# The Abacus from Russia

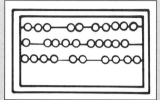

**Simple abacus**

**Figure 1**

**Y**ou may have seen little children playing with a toy that looks like **Figure 1**. It has a frame in the shape of a rectangle. Several wires hold rows of beads. Children love to move the beads back and forth and hear the clacking sounds as the beads bump together. This toy is called an abacus. But it is more than just a toy.

When I visited Russia a few years ago, I saw many calculators and computers. But I was surprised to see that people were also doing calculations with the abacus. The Russians call it a *scety* (SCHAW-tee) and use it as a counting board. In many Russian stores a scety lay next to the cash register. **Figure 2**

When Napoleon invaded Russia in 1812, a mathematician traveling with the French army saw Russian people using this type of abacus. What a wonderful way to teach arithmetic, he thought. He brought a scety back to France, where it became popular.

From there it spread to other European countries and to America.

Here is a scety showing the number 427.50. It may be the price of a television set or a fridge. Try to read the number. Here are some hints. **Figure 3**

- Count the number of beads on each wire. How many are dark? How many are light?
- Count the number of beads on the left side in each row. Write down the number for each row.
- How is the decimal point shown? How is zero shown?
- Now can you read the number 427.50 on the abacus?

You can make your own scety. Here are suggestions about the materials you will need.

## MATERIALS
- Heavy cardboard rectangle, about 8¹/₂ inches by 11 inches (21 cm by 27 cm)

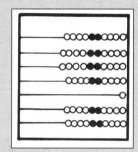

**Russian abacus**

**Figure 2**

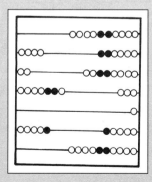

**Scety showing 427.50**

**Figure 3**

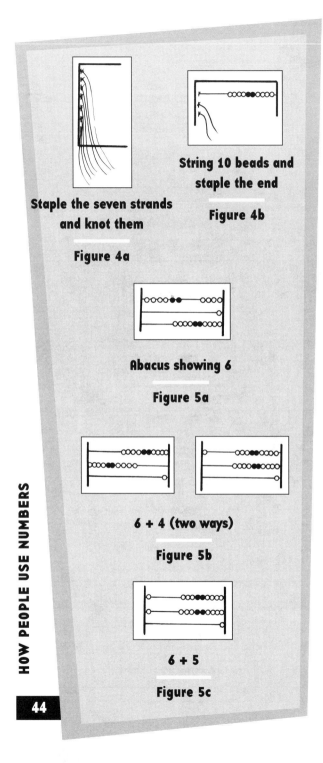

**Staple the seven strands and knot them**

**Figure 4a**

**String 10 beads and staple the end**

**Figure 4b**

**Abacus showing 6**

**Figure 5a**

**6 + 4 (two ways)**

**Figure 5b**

**6 + 5**

**Figure 5c**

- Thick string, enough to make seven rows and fasten the ends (about 7 feet, or 2 m, 10cm)
- Stapler
- Scissors
- Ruler
- 49 light-colored beads and 12 dark-colored beads (You might also use pieces of macaroni and color 12 pieces with a pen or marker.) Make sure you have enough space to move 10 beads or macaroni pieces on each string.

## MAKING A RUSSIAN ABACUS

**1.** Cut the string into seven equal pieces, each a little longer than the length of the cardboard.

**2.** Staple one end of each piece of string to the cardboard. Knot the string at the staple. **Figure 4a**

**3.** Start with the top string. Place four light beads, then two dark beads, then four more light beads on the string. Staple the end of the string to the cardboard. Knot the end of the string around the staple. **Figure 4b**

**4.** Do the same as in step 3 for each string, except for the decimal point string, which has just one light bead (see **Figure 2**).

Does your *scety* look like the one in **Figure 2**?

## THINGS TO THINK ABOUT AND DO

**1.** Show several different numbers on your scety.

**2.** Think how you would use your abacus to teach a child to add. Start with small numbers; for example: 6 + 2; 6 + 4 (two ways); 6 + 5. What do you do when all 10 beads on the string have been moved to the left? You exchange those 10 beads for a single bead on the next higher strand. Then you move the 10 beads on the lower string back to the starting position and continue. **Figure 5a**, **Figure 5b**, **Figure 5c**

**3.** Think how you would teach a child to subtract on the abacus. Then try your method.

**4.** How does the abacus help children to learn arithmetic? What are the disadvantages?

**5.** Pretend you are a clerk in a Russian store. Use your abacus to add and subtract larger numbers, showing dollars and cents.

# The Abacus from China

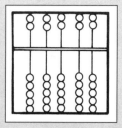

**Chinese abacus**

**Figure 6**

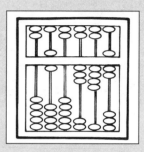

**Suan pan showing 60,347**

**Figure 7**

Counting boards have been in use for thousands of years. People laid sticks or pebbles on a board in columns to show ones, tens, hundreds, and higher numbers. The word *calculate* comes from the Latin word *calculus*, meaning "pebble." Two thousand years ago the Romans, who spoke Latin, were doing arithmetic with pebbles on a counting board. At some point, a smart person thought of stringing beads on cords or wires and fastening them to a wooden frame. That's how the abacus was born.

The Chinese abacus, called a *suan pan* (SWAN PAN) dates back about eight centuries. The name *suan pan* means "counting board." You may have seen such an abacus in Chinese shops or restaurants. It lies flat on a counter or table. **Figure 6**

Each strand has seven beads. Five are below the crossbar and two are above it. Each bead above the crossbar has the same value as five beads on the lower part of the wire. Think of five fingers representing a hand. Ten fingers are equal to two hands. The two upper beads together represent ten of the lower beads.

The suan pan in **Figure 7** shows the number 60,347. Can you see how it works? It has place value, just like our number system—ones, tens, hundreds, and higher numbers. To show a number, push the beads toward the crossbar.

You can make your own five-column suan pan.

## MATERIALS

- Use the same materials as for the Russian abacus (page 43), with these differences:
- About 50 inches (1.25 m = 125 cm) of string
- 35 beads
- Sticky tape (optional)

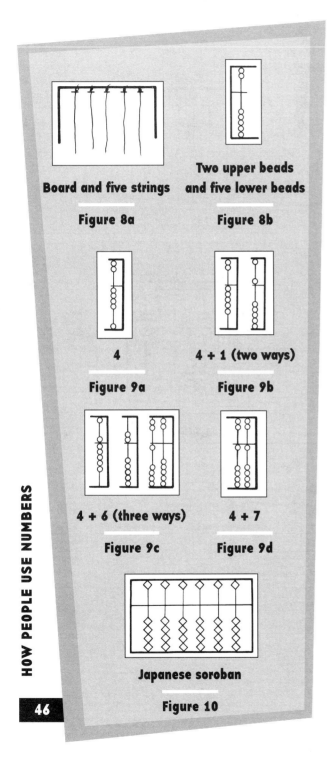

**Board and five strings**

Figure 8a

**Two upper beads and five lower beads**

Figure 8b

**4**

Figure 9a

**4 + 1 (two ways)**

Figure 9b

**4 + 6 (three ways)**

Figure 9c

**4 + 7**

Figure 9d

**Japanese soroban**

Figure 10

## MAKING A CHINESE ABACUS

**1.** Cut the string into five pieces, each a little longer than the width of the cardboard.

**2.** Staple the end of each string to the cardboard and knot it at the staple. **Figure 8a**

**3.** Start with the first string. Place two beads on it and staple or tape the string so that the beads can be moved. The staple or tape serves as a crossbar.

**4.** Place five beads on the string. Staple the end of the string to the cardboard and knot it. **Figure 8b**

**5.** Do the same as in step 3 and step 4 with the remaining beads and pieces of string.

Does your suan pan look like the one in **Figure 6**?

## THINGS TO THINK ABOUT AND DO

**1.** Show several large numbers on your suan pan.

**2.** Practice adding small numbers on the suan pan. Try these examples:

Start with 4. Then show 4 + 1 (two ways); 4 + 2; 4 + 6 (three ways); 4 + 7 **Figure 9a**, **Figure 9b**, **Figure 9c**, **Figure 9d**

**3.** Compare the Chinese abacus with the Russian abacus. Which is easier to learn? Which is faster to operate? Which is easier to read?

**4.** The Japanese adopted the Chinese abacus four or five hundred years ago. Then they made some changes. Instead of two beads above the crossbar, they had only one bead, representing five of the beads below the crossbar. Later, some Japanese started to use an abacus with only four beads below the crossbar. The Japanese call their abacus a soroban. **Figure 10**

You might think that working with a soroban is rather slow. Japanese children start to use the soroban when they are very young, and they learn to do much of the calculation in their heads. The soroban can even beat the calculator for some types of calculations.

You can make your own soroban!

# The Calendar of the Iroquois of North America

Suppose your birthday is coming up in a few weeks. You want to know on which day of the week it will fall. One way to find out is to look at a calendar. Usually a calendar is printed for a full year. It is divided into months, with a separate page for each month. Each month is divided into weeks of seven days each. How did people decide on these divisions of time, and why are they important?

Let's first think about the year. The farmer needs to plant the seeds at a certain time so that the crop will ripen properly. At what time of the year does it rain? When is it very hot or very cold? In ancient Egypt the priests observed the rising of the star Sirius, the Dog Star, and connected that event with the annual flooding of the Nile River. They figured that the year was a bit more than 365 days long.

Other people have looked to the moon to help them calculate the passage of time. Some years ago scientists found an ancient bone near the African village of Ishango, in the Democratic Republic of Congo. The bone had notches on it in a regular pattern. A scientist examined it under a microscope and decided that the notches marked the days of a six-month lunar calendar, one based on the cycles of the moon. This bone is about 25,000 years old! Just imagine, people were keeping track of time that long ago!

The Iroquois live in the northern part of New York State and in adjoining parts of Canada. They call themselves the *Haudenosaunee*, a name that means "people of the longhouse." The name *Iroquois* was given to them by the French. Long ago they worked out a calendar by watching both the moon and the sun, and perhaps certain stars. Their year had 13 moons. Each moon, or month, had 28 days.

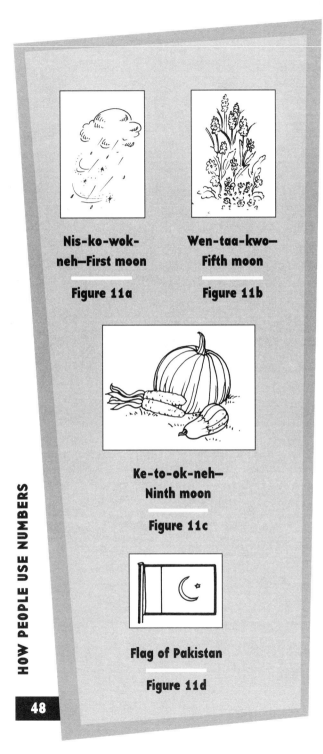

**Nis-ko-wok-neh—First moon**

Figure 11a

**Wen-taa-kwo—Fifth moon**

Figure 11b

**Ke-to-ok-neh—Ninth moon**

Figure 11c

**Flag of Pakistan**

Figure 11d

Each Iroquois moon had a name. The first moon was called *Nis-ko-wok-neh*, the moon of "snow and blizzards." The fifth moon was *Wen-taa-kwo*, "the flowers." The ninth moon was *Ke-to-ok-neh*, "the harvest." **Figure 11a**, **Figure 11b**, **Figure 11c**

People still use the moon to set dates for some holidays, such as Easter in the Christian calendar and Passover in the Hebrew calendar. In the twelfth century the Jewish scholar Moses Maimonides wrote a book called *On the Computation of the New Moon*. The Jews started each month with the appearance of the new moon. That's how they decided whether a month had 29 days or 30 days and were able to set the days of their holidays.

The Islamic calendar is based entirely on the cycles of the moon. It has 12 months of 29½ days, counting from one new moon to the next. Actually the months alternate between 29 days and 30 days.

## THINGS TO THINK ABOUT

**1.** How many days are in the Iroquois year? How many days are in the Islamic year? Which is longer, and by how many days? Compare them with our calendar year.

**2.** Name the months in our year that might have the names given to the Iroquois months.

**3.** We have many divisions of time. Think about these divisions: century, decade, year, month, week, day, hour, minute. Which were based on natural happenings? Which were invented by people?

**4.** Look at the flag of Pakistan, an Islamic country. It shows a crescent moon, the new moon. Why is that important? **Figure 11d**

## THINGS TO DO

**1.** The Iroquois call themselves the "people of the longhouse." Do research to find out why. See page 84 for a picture of the Iroquois longhouse.

**2.** Read the book *Thirteen Moons on Turtle's Back*, by the Abenaki writer Joseph Bruchac and the poet Jonathan London (see Bibliography on page 156).

**3.** Make a list of the months in our year. Give each month a name according to the weather or an important activity. Draw pictures to show what happens in each month.

# The Calendar of the Maya from Mexico and Central America

**Symbol for Day One**

**Figure 12a**

**Symbol for Day Two**

**Figure 12b**

**Symbol for Day Fifteen**

**Figure 12c**

For thousands of years the Maya have lived in the region that is now southern Mexico and northern Central America. The Maya were great astronomers. They devised their calendars more than 2,000 years ago. For everyday use they had a 365-day calendar. It consisted of 18 months of 20 days each, and five additional days. They also had a sacred calendar to keep track of holidays and religious observances. This calendar had 13 months of 20 days each.

The Maya built stone monuments that tell about their kings and important events. They also wrote books dealing with the sun, the moon, and the planets, especially Venus. Most of the books were destroyed by the Spanish conquerors in the sixteenth century because they considered these books to be "the work of the devil." These writings contain many dates. Sometimes a picture of a special head indicated a particular day of the month. **Figure 12a**, **Figure 12b**, **Figure 12c**

The Maya had an interesting way of showing a period of time in their writings and stone monuments. For this purpose they used a year that had 360 days—18 months of 20 days each. The number in **Figure 13** is 5 years, 13 months, 9 days.

This may seem a strange way to write a number. Here is the code for reading it:

Each dot stands for a unit. Each bar stands for five units. The position of the bars and dots is important in reading the number.

- The lowest position tells you the number of days: $5 + 4 = 9$ days.
- The next position tells you the number of months:
  $2 \times 5 + 3 = 13$ months, and
  $13 \times 20 = 260$ days.

**Figure 13**

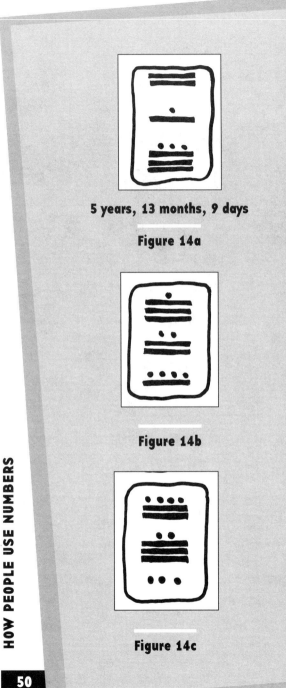

**5 years, 13 months, 9 days**

**Figure 14a**

**Figure 14b**

**Figure 14c**

- The highest position tells you the number of years: 5 years, and 5 × 360 = 1,800 days.
- The total number of days is 1,800 + 260 + 9 = 2,069 days.

Why did the Maya use bars and dots to write numbers? Probably the idea came from the marketplace. People figured out prices and money by laying out twigs and pebbles. A twig equaled five pebbles. In writing, a twig became a bar and a pebble became a dot.

The Maya had names for various units of time, as shown in this table:

| MAYA NAME | NUMBER OF DAYS |
|-----------|----------------|
| baktun | 20 × 7,200 = 144,000 |
| katun | 20 × 360 = 7,200 |
| tun | 18 × 20 = 360 |
| uinal | 20 × 1 = 20 |
| kin | 1 = 1 |

Some of their calendar stones show periods of time going back to a date that we call August 13, 3114 B.C.E. in our calendar. That's more than 5,000 years ago!

## THINGS TO THINK ABOUT AND DO

**1.** Calculate the number of days for the period of time in each of the three calendar stones in **Figure 14**. Then translate them into years, months, and days in our calendar. How will you treat leap years?

**2.** Teach a friend the Maya system of writing periods of time. Then write several calendar numbers for your friend to calculate.

**3.** Calculate the number of days in a calendar stone that shows: 2 katuns, 10 tuns, 6 uinals, 12 kins. Then draw the stone.

**4.** People usually started counting by using parts of their bodies, such as the ten fingers. That is why the number ten is so important in many counting systems. Why do you think the number twenty is important in the Maya system of numbers?

You may check some of the answers on page 153.

# Signs of the Zodiac from China

Thousands of years ago, the Chinese invented a lunar calendar, one based on the cycles of the moon. This calendar is still used to set the dates for the New Year and other festivals. The New Year occurs sometime in late January or early February, according to our calendar. You may have seen the colorful parades and floats that celebrate the Chinese New Year.

You may also have seen place mats in Chinese restaurants with pictures of the 12 animal signs. The calendar is based on a cyclical concept of time, a cycle of 12 years that repeats over and over again. Each year is associated with an animal, in the following order: Rat, Ox, Tiger, Rabbit, Dragon, Snake, Horse, Sheep, Monkey, Rooster, Dog, Pig. Each animal was supposed to be associated with a certain type of personality and achievement in life.

Why does the Rat come first? According to the folk tale, the animals were quarreling about who should be the leader. They decided that they would all swim across the river, and the first to come ashore would lead the rest. But the clever Rat rode on the back of the Ox. Just as the Ox was reaching the shore, the Rat jumped off. That is why the Rat comes first in the cycle. The Pig was lazy and came in last.

You can make your own mat with a Chinese Zodiac design.

## MATERIALS
- Compass (If you don't have a compass, you can attach a pencil to a piece of string.)
- Sheet of white paper, at least 8 inches (20 cm) square
- Sheet of colored construction paper, larger than the white sheet

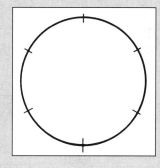

**Figure 15a**

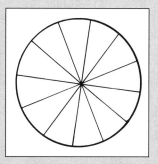

**Figure 15b**

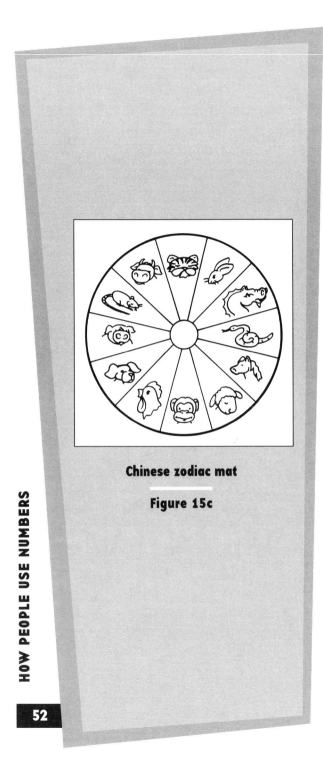

**Chinese zodiac mat**

**Figure 15c**

- Ruler
- Pencil
- Crayons or markers of several colors
- Glue

## MAKING THE CHINESE ZODIAC MAT

**1.** Draw a large circle on the white paper.

**2.** Use the same radius, and mark off six arcs on the circle. **Figure 15a**

**3.** Draw diameters—lines through the center of the circle—connecting the arcs.

**4.** Mark off six more points halfway between the first set and draw the diameters to connect them. **Figure 15b**

**5.** Draw and color the appropriate animal in each sector of the circle. **Figure 15c**

**6.** Glue the paper to the center of the mat.

**7.** Decorate the border of the mat.

## THINGS TO THINK ABOUT AND DO

**1.** The years of the Monkey are 1968, 1980, 1992, and 2004. The years of the Rooster are 1969, 1981, 1993, 2005. Make a list of the years for each animal, starting with the Rat in 1960.

**2.** Ask your friends in what year they were born. Do friends born in the same year have similar personalities?

**3.** Suppose your friend says he or she was born in the year of the Rooster. How old is your friend? Remember that the Chinese New Year starts in late January or early February.

**4.** Thousands of years ago people in the Middle East and Egypt looked up at the sky and saw the stars and the planets. They imagined that these formed certain figures—a goat, a ram, a fish—a total of 12, one for each month of the year. They divided the sky into 12 sectors, each having a named sign. Today they are known by their Latin names. I was born in the month of Capricorn, the Goat. Look up more information about these signs of the zodiac. Do you think they influence a person's life? Why or why not?

# Wampum, Cocoa Beans, and Pieces of Eight from American Colonies

When do you use money? When I was a child, we used metal coins and paper bills almost every time we bought something—ice cream, food, clothing. Today many people use coins and bills only to buy inexpensive items, such as a newspaper. For larger items they use credit cards and checks. Many people do their shopping on-line using credit cards. I can pay my credit card bill on-line, too. This is called electronic transfer.

Before there was money, people would barter one type of goods for another type. The farmer might exchange the corn he grew for the blacksmith's metal axe. But suppose the farmer didn't need an axe or the blacksmith already had enough corn. That's when money became necessary.

The first type of money was in the form of objects that had value in themselves. For example, the Iroquois made shell beads called wampum. A design made of wampum beads might have a certain message. Some museums have wampum belts that record treaties between nations. One such treaty is between the thirteen North American colonies and the six Iroquois nations, declaring peace between them. **Figure 16a**

Later the Iroquois sold fur pelts to European colonists for strings of wampum beads. The colonists also

**Washington Covenant Belt**

**Figure 16a**

Source: LeRoy H. Appleton. *American Indian Design and Decoration.*

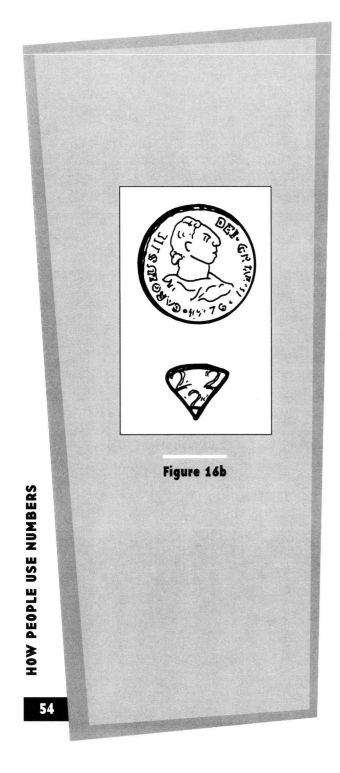

**Figure 16b**

used wampum as their money.

The Iroquois and other Native Americans owned and worked their land in common. They believed that land was for the use of all the people in the group and could not be owned by one person. The colonists had a different idea. The Native Americans didn't realize they were giving up the right to use the land when they accepted gifts of money, beads, or other items from the Europeans.

When the Spanish conquerors reached Mexico in 1519, they found that the Aztecs were using cocoa beans as currency. The largest unit was a bag of 8,000 beans. In the Aztec number system, as in that of the Maya (see page 49), twenty was the most important number.

The Spanish came to America looking for gold and silver, and they found what they were looking for. In 1536 they set up the first American mint in Mexico, and made the silver

coin worth eight *reales* (ray-AL-ays). These coins became the most widely used coins throughout the world and were often stolen by pirates. The coins were also called "Spanish dollars" or "pieces of eight," and were legal in the United States until 1857. If people needed smaller coins, they would cut up a silver dollar. A fourth of the coin was called "two bits," or two pieces out of the eight. Later they used the same name for one-fourth of a U.S. dollar. **Figure 16b**

## THINGS TO THINK ABOUT AND DO

**1.** Suppose a beaver pelt costs four strings of wampum beads and an otter pelt costs three strings. Find the cost of:

   **a.** Six beaver and four otter pelts. Figure it out in your head, as the Iroquois did.

   **b.** 25 beaver and 22 otter pelts. Can you do that mentally?

**2.** What other items did the Native Americans exchange with the colonists?

**3.** You may have read that the Dutch bought the island of Manhattan, now part of New York City, from the Manhatta Indians in 1626. What did each side of the exchange think about this sale? Imagine that you are a Manhatta Indian. How would you feel? Then put yourself in the place of a Dutch boy or girl who had just crossed the Atlantic Ocean looking for a new home.

**4.** Why would the Aztecs use a bag of 8,000 cocoa beans as their largest unit of money? How is this number related to twenty, the most important number in their system? Think how ten is related to 1,000 in our system.

**5.** Years ago there was a song that went: "Shave and a haircut, two bits!" What U.S. coin is worth "two bits"? Why? How many bits equal $1.50?

   You will find some answers on page 153.

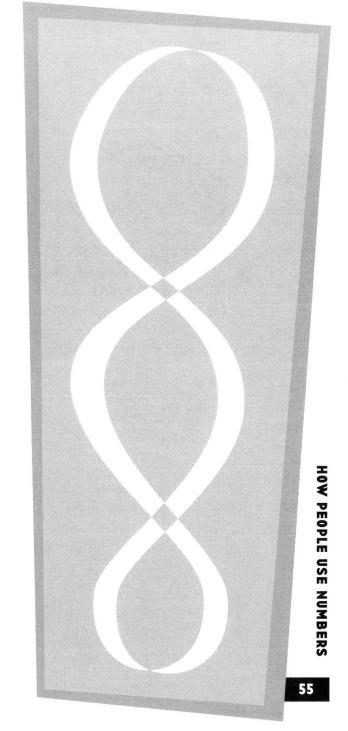

# Beads, Shells, and Gold from Africa

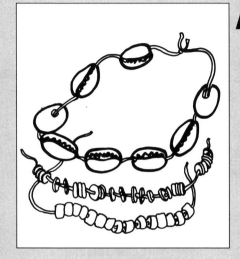

**Cowrie shells, trade beads, and ivory disks**

**Figure 17a**

If you had lived in West Africa a hundred years ago, you might have bought a chicken for several strings of cowrie shells. In fact, one name for 200 cowrie shells was *gallina*, from the Portuguese word for "hen." Cowries were very useful. They decorated all sorts of objects, were used in hairstyles and jewelry, and served as counters in the Mankala game. They were most useful as money. Some traders liked shell money better than gold even though it took a large quantity of shells to equal one gold coin in value. African merchants had a reputation for doing mental arithmetic with large numbers and remembering sales figures for years.

In parts of Central and East Africa, beads were used as money. They might be strung in groups of five or twenty. They were imported from Europe or made by the Africans themselves from ivory or ostrich egg shells. **Figure 17a**

A thousand years ago the richest person in the world was probably the king of the ancient West African kingdom of Ghana. It lies north of the modern country of Ghana. Another fabulous king was Mansa Musa, ruler of ancient Mali in West Africa. In 1324 he traveled to Egypt with 60,000 men and a fortune in gold. At this time African gold mines were furnishing the gold for Europe's currency.

By the year 1600 the Asante traders of Ghana had developed systems of brass weights to measure gold dust. These weights represented all types of people, animals, and objects, including even a board for the Mankala game. **Figure 17b**

## HOW TO BE AN AFRICAN MERCHANT IN THE NINETEENTH CENTURY

**1.** In the Congo region of Africa, beads were used as currency, as follows:

5 beads = 1 string
5 strings = 1 matanu (tanu means "five")

You paid 4 matanu, 2 strings, and 3 beads for a length of cloth. What was the cost of the cloth in beads? Do the calculations mentally, as the African merchants did.

**2.** When I was in Nigeria, I used Nigerian coins to buy a string of 40 cowrie shells and an iron manila, also used as currency long ago. **Figure 17c**

A century or more ago, these were the ratios of the various quantities of cowrie money:

40 cowries = 1 string
5 strings = 1 bunch
10 bunches = 1 head
10 heads = 1 bag

How many cowries are in one bag? A bag is as large a load as a man can carry. Try to do the calculations in your head, as the West African traders do. Many of these traders are women with very little schooling, but they can compute the largest sums mentally.

## THINGS TO THINK ABOUT AND DO

**1.** Get together with your friends to act out a market scene in West Africa in the nineteenth century. Pretend to use cowries as currency. Macaroni shells make good substitutes.

**2.** Some European traders liked cowrie shell money better than European gold coins. Think of some reasons for and against this preference.

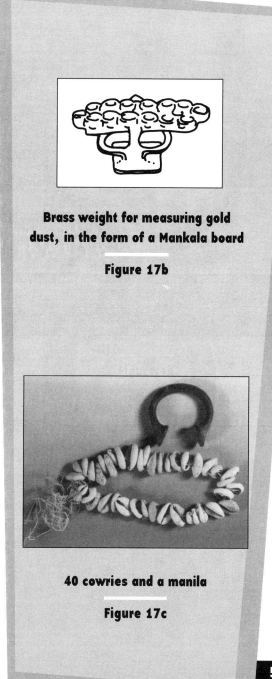

**Brass weight for measuring gold dust, in the form of a Mankala board**

**Figure 17b**

**40 cowries and a manila**

**Figure 17c**

# Save Those Cans! *from the* **United States**

L et's face it. People waste a lot of stuff—water, paper, food, cans. If we're not careful, the world may run short of these things one day.

People are now learning to recycle aluminum soda cans. This is really important. Do you know how much energy goes into making one soda can? Here are some numbers.

- The United States used about 65 billion aluminum soda cans in 1990.
- Throwing away one can wastes six ounces of gasoline.
- Energy saved by recycling one can will keep a television set running for three hours.

## THINGS TO THINK ABOUT AND DO

You may want to use a calculator for the first three steps. (You may check your answers on page 153.)

**1.** There were about 250 million people in the United States in 1990. How many soda cans did each person use, on the average?

**2.** Assume there were 200 million television sets in the United States. How many days would they run on the energy saved by recycling all soda cans in 1990?

**3.** There are 128 ounces in a gallon. How many gallons of gasoline would be saved per year if all cans were recycled?

**4.** Discuss with your friends or with your classmates a project for recycling soda cans. You might gather statistics on the number of cans your group and their families use, or are sold in school or in the local supermarket. How many are recycled? Make graphs and posters to illustrate your work.

**5.** Work with your friends to do a similar recycling project with another material, such as paper.

**6.** Read *Fifty Simple Things Kids Can Do to Save the Earth*, by the Earthworks Group (see Bibliography page 157), or a similar book about saving the environment.

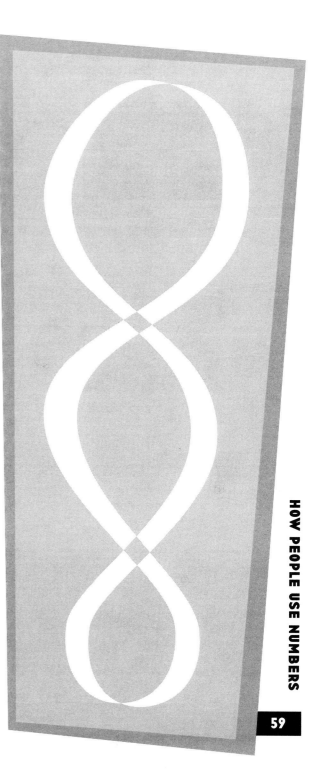

# Saving the Lives of Children Throughout the World

Recently I received a shocking announcement in the mail. It said: "Some 5,000 children die every day for want of a five-cent packet." The announcement came from the United States Fund for UNICEF, the United Nations Children's Fund.

What is this wonderful packet that costs only five cents? How does it save a child's life? The packet is a simple mixture of salts, sugar, and clean water. It is used to cure dehydration, the drying up of the body due to severe diarrhea. Doctors call the treatment oral rehydration therapy, or ORT. Parents call it a miracle that can save their children's lives.

ORT saves the lives of about two million children every year. But there are many sick children who do not get treatment. It may be difficult to reach them, or their parents may not know about the treatment, or their governments don't have the money to carry out the program. All of these things require money—for education, for travel to distant places, for doctors and nurses.

UNICEF helps children in many other ways. Here are some of the things that money can buy to help the children of the world:

- **Four cents will buy a year's supply of vitamin A supplements to fight blindness.**
- **$15 will buy enough seeds to grow over 1,600 pounds of nutritious food.**
- **$60 can provide warm sweaters and winter boots for 10 refugee children.**

## THINGS TO THINK ABOUT AND DO

**1.** Suppose your class can raise $100 for UNICEF. Figure out how many ORT packets can be bought for that amount of money. Do the same for vitamin A, warm clothes, and seeds. Try to do the calculations mentally or use a calculator. You may check your answers on page 153.

**2.** Discuss a project to raise money for UNICEF with your friends and classmates. You may contact the U.S. Committee for UNICEF at 333 East 38th Street, New York, NY 10016; telephone 1-800-FOR-KIDS; www.unicefusa.org. UNICEF will send kits for fund-raising.

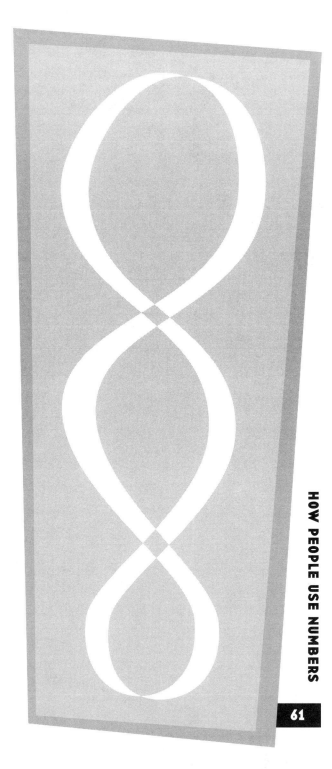

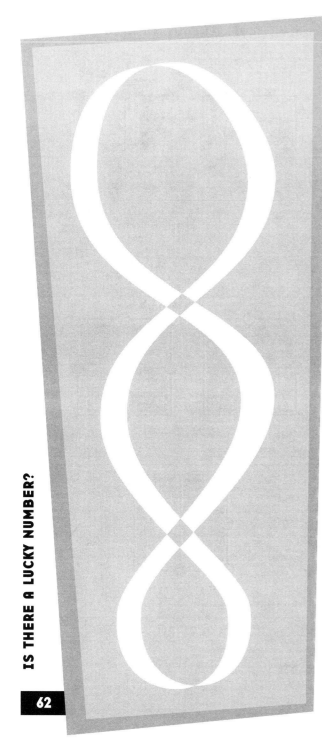

# 4

# Is There a Lucky Number?

Since the time when people first learned to count, they have chosen certain numbers as special. To the early Greeks of the school of Pythagoras, numbers were very important. They considered even numbers to be female and odd numbers male. To the wise men of Mesopotamia we owe our seven-day week. They saw seven "wandering stars" in the sky. Many Native Americans regard the Four Directions as special. And how many Americans even today think the number thirteen is unlucky?

Magic squares have a long history going back thousands of years to ancient China. In India and parts of Africa, people wore them as charms to ward off evil. Medicine men of ancient Persia thought they could cure illness. They were part of the religion of Islam at certain times. Mathematicians in all parts of the world have studied magic squares and their special properties. They constructed larger and larger magic squares, some with borders of numbers. Books have been written about them. Even Benjamin Franklin tried his hand at them. You will learn about some of the simpler types of magic squares. Perhaps this will make you want to learn more about them.

# Thirteen— Lucky or Unlucky? from the U.S.A.

"Do you know that tomorrow is Friday the thirteenth?" Eddie told his friends.

"So what?" asked Sam.

Disgusted, Eddie said: "So what! It's Friday the *thirteenth*! Bad luck!"

"That's nonsense. It's just superstition, about any special number being unlucky. Just to show you, I will write 'Friday the 13th' on this paper and put it in my pocket tomorrow. You'll see, nothing bad will happen to me." Sam wrote the message and took it home to put in his shirt pocket the following day.

Everything went smoothly on Friday. Sam checked his pocket every once in a while to make sure the message was there. Just as the family was getting ready to eat supper, Sam's mother noticed that there was no bread. She sent Sam out to buy a loaf. "And don't waste time on your way back home!" she called out as he was leaving.

Sam ran to the bakery. He was so hungry, he could hardly wait to get home and eat. He grabbed the loaf and ran across the street just as a car was approaching. The car driver saw him and slowed down but not soon enough. The car hit Sam and knocked him down before it could completely stop. But Sam was able to scramble to his feet. He told the driver he was OK and ran home with the bread. He didn't say a word to his family about his accident.

Soon after supper he began to feel faint. His mother noticed how pale he was and became alarmed. Finally Sam told his family what happened. Immediately they called the doctor. After an examination, the doctor said: "He had a bad shock, but no damage. Don't worry, he'll be OK. Put him to bed, and he will be fine in the morning."

Meanwhile word of the accident spread around the neighborhood.

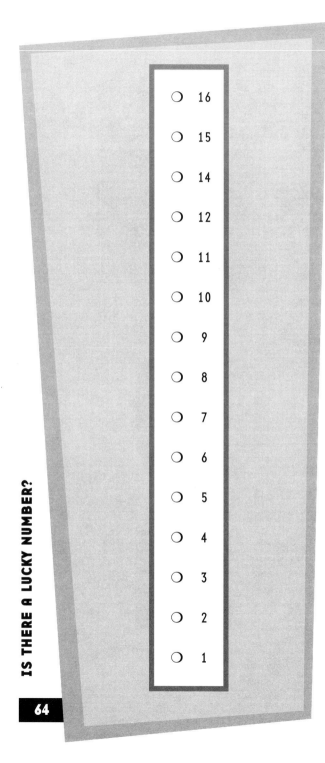

Soon Eddie and the other boys arrived at Sam's house to find out how he was.

"I told you Friday the thirteenth was unlucky!" Eddie exclaimed.

Sam shot back: "How do you know? If I hadn't carried this paper with Friday the 13th written on it, I might have been killed!"

## THINGS TO THINK ABOUT AND DO

**1.** The story about Sam is true. Sam is my husband. This happened to him when he was 11 years old. Do you think that Friday the thirteenth had anything to do with Sam's accident? Did the paper with the words "Friday the 13th" make a difference in the outcome of the accident?

**2.** Many tall buildings number the floors "10, 11, 12, 14," skipping the number 13. I live on the thirteenth floor of my apartment house. My building does not skip 13. When I took the apartment, the building manager shook my hand and congratulated me for my fearlessness! There is a name for fear of thirteen. It is *triskaidekaphobia*. Look up the word in the dictionary to find out the origin.

**3.** The United States was formed from the 13 colonies. That is why the flag has 13 stripes. Look at the back of a dollar bill. Count the steps of the pyramid. Count the leaves on the olive branch that the eagle is holding. The number in each case is 13. Can you find other groups of 13 on the back of the dollar bill?

**4.** For the Maya of Mexico and Central America, thirteen was a special number. Their sacred calendar had thirteen months (see page 49). Find other examples of thirteen as a special number.

**5.** Ask your friends what they think about the number thirteen. If they are afraid of it, ask them why.

# Seven— Lucky or Unlucky? from the Ancient World

The wise men of ancient Mesopotamia (now Iraq) looked up at the sky night after night. They noticed that some heavenly bodies scarcely changed their position, while others seemed to move around the earth. They counted seven moving objects in the sky—the sun, the moon, and five planets—and named them the "wandering stars." People thought these bodies were the messengers of the gods. They named the days of the week after them. That is why we have a seven-day week, although the names have changed.

People speak of the Seven Wonders of the Ancient World. One was the Pyramid for the king Khufu in Egypt, dating to 2650 B.C.E. (Before the Common Era). Another was the Colossus statue in Rhodes, so gigantic that a ship could pass between its legs. The Hanging Gardens in Babylon was another wonder. Most likely, other wonderful objects existed in the ancient world, but seven were chosen because the number seven was considered lucky.

The number seven has remained a special number through the ages. Let's go back to ancient Egypt. In a papyrus written about 1650 B.C.E., the scribe Ahmes wrote the following list, using Egyptian numerals:

| | |
|---|---|
| Houses | 7 |
| Cats | 49 |
| Mice | 343 |
| Heads of wheat | 2,401 |
| Hekats of grain | 16,807 |
| Total | 19,607 |

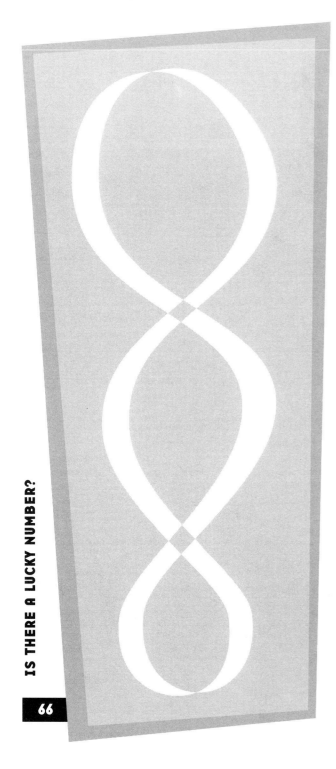

This list may seem like a mystery. We can check that each number is seven times the number before it. But what does it all mean?

Let's move forward in time to the year 1202. In a book by the Italian mathematician Leonardo Fibonacci appears this puzzle:

**Seven old women are on the road to Rome. Each woman has 7 mules, each mule carries 7 sacks, each sack holds 7 loaves, for each loaf there are 7 knives, and each knife is in 7 sheaths. How many objects are there: women, mules, sacks, loaves, knives, and sheaths?**

Ahmes probably had something like that in mind but didn't write it out in words. His puzzle might go like this:

A person owns 7 houses. In each house live 7 cats. Each cat killed 7 mice. Each mouse ate 7 heads of wheat. Each head of wheat would give 7 hekats of grain. How many objects are there altogether?

Now move forward in time another 600 years to 1802. Here is a popular children's verse from England at this time:

As I was going to St. Ives
I met a man with seven wives.
Every wife had seven sacks,
Every sack had seven cats,
Every cat had seven kits.
Kits, cats, sacks, and wives,
How many were going to
St. Ives?

This is a trick puzzle. If the speaker was going to St. Ives, but the man he met was going in the opposite direction, the answer is "one."

## THINGS TO THINK ABOUT AND DO

**1.** Think about the names of the days of the week. Sunday is named after the sun. Find out the origin of the names of the other six days. Look in your dictionary or ask your school librarian for help. Some of the days are named after Norse gods.

**2.** Research the Seven Wonders of the World. What are they? What happened to them? The pyramid in Egypt is the only Wonder that we can still visit today. If you were asked to name Seven Wonders of the world we live in, what would you name?

**3.** Check the arithmetic in Ahmes's puzzle. Was he correct?

**4.** With his book, published in 1202, Leonardo Fibonacci introduced Indo-Arabic numerals to Europe. These are the numerals we use now. What kind of numerals did Europeans use before then?

**5.** Suppose you roll two dice. What number combination would you bet on? Show that seven comes up more often than any other combination. (The faces of a die are numbered one to six.) For example, you might have one on the first die and six on the second die. You should find six combinations that add up to seven. How many combinations add up to six? to eight?

# Letters and Numbers from Europe

For many centuries, before they learned the Indo-Arabic numerals we use now, Europeans used Roman numerals. Of course, they are clumsy when you have to do calculations. But they are very useful when you want to connect numbers and letters.

In ancient and medieval times, Jews used the letters of the Hebrew alphabet as symbols for numbers. But they had a taboo on writing the name of Jehovah. One way to spell the name was the combination *yod heh*. This combination also stood for fifteen—ten and five. So they solved the problem by using the combination nine plus six for fifteen.

Some Jews, and later some Christians, thought they could predict the future or describe the character of a person by adding the values of the letters in a word or name. This practice is called Gematria (gah-MAH-tree-ah). That's how some people came to be labeled the "beast." This is how it worked.

Find the value of the Roman number DCLXVI. Notice that each letter, representing

| D | C | L | X | V | I |
|---|---|---|---|---|---|
| 500 | 100 | 50 | 10 | 5 | 1 |

is used just once. This number, 666, was considered the "number of the beast." It was used to attack people who were disliked. This is how it might work. Spell the person's name. Cross out all the letters that are not used to write Roman numbers. Add some letters—make up a reason to do that. Rearrange the letters. If you are clever, you can make the letters spell out DCLXVI. In the struggle between Catholics and Protestants in the sixteenth century, both Pope Leo X and Martin Luther were labeled the "beast" by their opponents. In the same way, Julius Caesar and Napoleon became the "beast."

## THE LETTER-NUMBER GAME

Play this game with your friends, using letters as numbers.

**1.** Write the numbers from 1 to 9 in a column along the left side of a sheet of paper. Make up a personality trait for each of the numbers. For example: 1 = Cheerful; 2 = Helpful; and so on.

**2.** Write the letters of the alphabet across the page. Write the numbers 1 to 26 under the letters.

```
A    B    C    ...    X    Y    Z
1    2    3    ...    24   25   26
```

**3.** Add the values of the letters in your name. If the sum has more than one digit, add those digits. Repeat the process until the final sum has just one digit.

**4.** Check that digit with the list of personality traits. Does it describe your personality?

For example, look at the name Ann.

```
A = 1, N = 14
1 + 14 + 14 = 29 → 11 → 2
2 = Helpful
```

## THINGS TO THINK ABOUT AND DO

Different numbers are considered special in various societies. What can you find out about them?

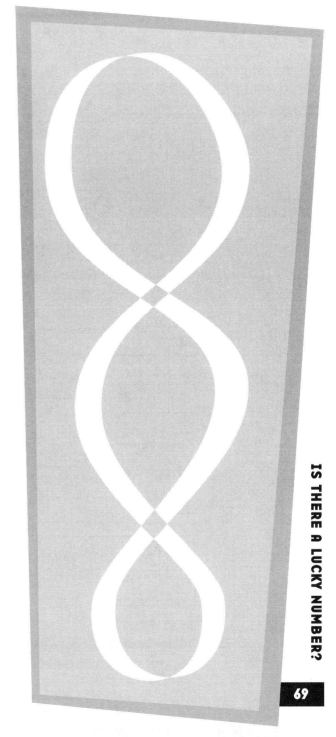

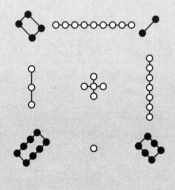

**Lo Shu**

**Figure 1a**

| 4 | 9 | 2 |
|---|---|---|
| 3 | 5 | 7 |
| 8 | 1 | 6 |

**Magic square**

**Figure 1b**

**Magic square in East Arabic numerals**

**Figure 2**

# Magic Squares from China and the Muslim World

The Chinese may have invented magic squares. They tell this story: About 4,000 years ago the emperor and his court were sailing down the River Lo. Suddenly a turtle appeared out of the water. On the turtle's back was the design you see here. When they looked at it carefully, they saw that nine numbers were in the design. They called the design of numbers the *Lo Shu*, which means "river map." **Figure 1a**, **Figure 1b**

- Add each row across. The sum is 15.
- Add each column going down. The sum is 15.
- Add each diagonal. The sum is 15.
- The number 15 is the magic sum for this magic square.

The art of making magic squares spread to other lands—to India and Japan, to the Middle East, to Africa, and finally to Europe and America. In the Middle East and Africa magic squares became part of Islam, the religion of the Muslims.

Muslim scholars enjoyed making large, complicated magic squares. They called this the "science of secrets." They wrote in East Arabic numerals. Very often they would introduce mistakes on purpose, to keep ordinary people from learning the science. Perhaps these squares were a code to send secret messages! In the eighteenth century the Nigerian scholar Muhammad ibn Muhammad wrote a whole book in Arabic about magic squares.

This magic square uses the numbers 1 to 9 once each. The magic sum is 15. **Figure 2**

## MATERIALS

- Paper (lined paper is best)
- Pencil
- Eraser
- Ruler

## THINGS TO THINK ABOUT AND DO

**1.** Analyze the magic square in **Figure 1b**. What number is in the center? How is this number related to the magic sum 15? What is the sum of all the numbers in the square? How is this sum related to the center number? What type of numbers are in the corners? With these hints in mind, draw your own magic square. Place the number 1 in the center of the top row, then complete the square.

**2.** Draw a square and divide it into nine spaces. Translate the East Arabic square into our Indo-Arabic numerals. Two spaces have been filled in to help you get started. **Figure 3**

**3.** Make a chart. Write the numbers from 1 to 9 across a page. Under each number, write the matching East Arabic numeral.

**4.** Use your chart in step 3 to translate the two magic squares in **Figure 4a** and **4b**

You may check some of your answers on page 153.

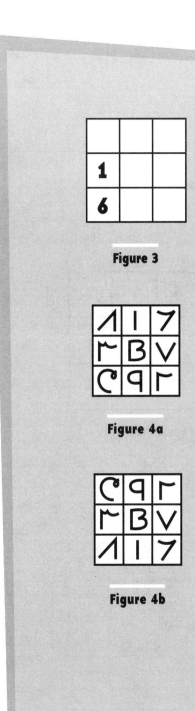

**Figure 3**

**Figure 4a**

**Figure 4b**

# Playing with Magic Squares for Everybody

| 4 | 9 | 2 |
|---|---|---|
| 3 | 5 | 7 |
| 8 | 1 | 6 |

**Basic magic square**

**Figure 5**

In the last activity you made $3 \times 3$ magic squares with the numbers 1 to 9. The center number was 5. The magic sum was $3 \times 5$ or 15. The even numbers were in the corners of the square.

Suppose you want to make a magic square using the numbers 2 to 10. All you have to do is add a 1 to each number in the magic square you already made. Before you do that, figure out what the magic sum should be. If you add a 1 to each number in a row, the magic sum should be $15 + 3$ or 18. The center number is even and the numbers in the corners are odd.

## CHANGING MAGIC SQUARES
## MATERIALS
- Sheet of paper. If you have centimeter or $1/2$-inch graph paper, that would be helpful. Lined paper is also good.
- Pencil
- Eraser
- Ruler

## MAKING THE MAGIC SQUARES

**1.** Draw several squares, divided into nine small squares.

**2.** Copy a magic square in the previous activity, or use this basic magic square. **Figure 5**

**3.** Make a new magic square using the numbers 2 to 10. What is the magic sum? What is the center number?

**4.** Make another magic square using the even numbers from 2 to 18. Before you make the square, figure out what number to put in the center. What magic sum do you expect?

## THINGS TO THINK ABOUT AND DO

**1.** Suppose you take the basic magic square and multiply each number by three. What is the magic sum? What number goes in the center? What is the sum of all the numbers? Check your work by making the magic square.

**2.** Suppose you add 5 to each number in the basic magic square. What is the center number? What is the magic sum? What is the sum of all the numbers? Make the magic square and check your answers.

**3.** Choose any page of a monthly calendar. Draw a square around a 3 × 3 block of nine numbers. **Figure 6**

Rearrange these nine numbers to form a magic square. Here is a hint: the center number remains the same. If it is even, the corner numbers are odd; if it is odd, the corner numbers are even.

What is the sum of all the numbers? How is it related to the center number?

**4.** Muslim scholars purposely wrote magic squares with mistakes. Find the mistake in this magic square. The magic sum is 30. **Figure 7**

**June**

| 1 | 2 | 3 | 4 | 5 | 6 | 7 |
|---|---|---|---|---|---|---|
| 8 | 9 | 10 | 11 | 12 | 13 | 14 |
| 15 | 16 | 17 | 18 | 19 | 20 | 21 |
| 22 | 23 | 24 | 25 | 26 | 27 | 28 |
| 29 | 30 | | | | | |

**Calendar square**

**Figure 6**

| 3 | 16 | 11 |
|---|---|---|
| 18 | 10 | 2 |
| 9 | 14 | 17 |

**Find the mistake**

**Figure 7**

# Four-by-Four Magic Squares from Europe

| 16 | 3 | 2 | 13 |
|----|----|----|----|
| 5 | 10 | 11 | 8 |
| 9 | 6 | 7 | 12 |
| 4 | 15 | 14 | 1 |

**Dürer's magic square**

**Figure 8**

This magic square appears in a famous painting called *Melancholia*, meaning "sadness." A four-by-four magic square is called the "square of Jupiter," the Roman god who is supposed to represent humor. Perhaps Albrecht Dürer, the great German artist, wanted to help someone get over a feeling of depression. In the bottom row you see 15 and 14. Dürer painted the picture in the year 1514. **Figure 8**

## THINGS TO FIGURE OUT

**1.** Copy Dürer's magic square. What numbers did Dürer use?

**2.** Find the sum of each row. Find the sum of each column. Find the sum of each diagonal. This sum is called the *magic number*.

**3.** Look at the 2 × 2 square in the upper left. What is the sum of the four numbers: 16, 3, 5, and 10? Find the sum of the four numbers in the upper right square, in the lower left square, and in the lower right square. Did you get the same answer every time?

**4.** Find the sum of the four numbers in the 2 × 2 square in the center.

**5.** The magic number for this 4 × 4 square is 34. Can you find other ways to add four numbers to get the magic number? One way is to add 16, 2, 7, and 9. If you draw lines connecting these numbers, they form a 3 × 3 square. Add the numbers in the corners of other 3 × 3 squares.

**6.** Connect the numbers 3, 5, 14, and 12 to form a parallelogram. Find the sum of the numbers. Can you draw other parallelograms by connecting four numbers so that the sum is 34?

You can construct a 4 × 4 magic square. Here is a way to make one using all the numbers from 1 to 16 exactly once each.

## MATERIALS

- Sheet of paper. If you have centimeter or half-inch graph paper, you won't have to draw lines.
- Pencil
- Eraser
- Ruler

## CONSTRUCTING THE MAGIC SQUARE

**1.** Draw two 4 × 4 squares, each divided into 16 small squares.

**2.** Write the numbers 1 to 16 in the first square. **Figure 9a**

**3.** In the second square, write the numbers in the two diagonals in the opposite order.

**4.** Copy the remaining numbers from the first square in the same order. **Figure 9b**

**5.** Check that the magic sum is 34. Find the sum of the four numbers in each 2 × 2 square. Look for other ways to get the sum 34 by adding four numbers.

**6.** Compare your magic square with the square in the Dürer painting.

## THINGS TO DO

Look at a monthly calendar. Choose a 4 × 4 square of numbers. Copy this square of numbers. Rearrange the 16 numbers to form a magic square. Why does it work?

| 1 | 2 | 3 | 4 |
|---|---|---|---|
| 5 | 6 | 7 | 8 |
| 9 | 10 | 11 | 12 |
| 13 | 14 | 15 | 16 |

**Starting array**

Figure 9a

| 16 | 2 | 3 | 13 |
|---|---|---|---|
|  | 11 | 10 |  |
|  | 7 | 6 |  |
| 4 |  |  | 1 |

**Making a 4 x 4 magic square**

Figure 9b

# Panmagic Magic Squares

| 1 | 12 | 7 | 14 |
|---|----|----|----|
| 8 | 13 | 2 | 11 |
| 10 | 3 | 16 | 5 |
| 15 | 6 | 9 | 4 |

**Panmagic magic square**

**Figure 10a**

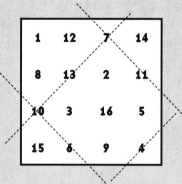

**Add the numbers in the broken diagonals**

**Figure 10b**

There are several different names for this type of 4 × 4 magic square. *Panmagic* means that it is magic in many different ways. It is also called *diabolical*, meaning "connected to the devil."

Other names are *perfect* and *pandiagonal*. The word *pandiagonal* tells you why this type of magic square is special. It means that you can get the magic sum, 34, by adding the numbers in broken diagonals, besides all the other ways described in the previous activity. There are 48 different magic squares using the numbers from 1 to 16 that have this feature. **Figure 10a** is one example.

## THINGS TO THINK ABOUT AND DO

**1.** Copy the magic square (**Figure 10a**). See the list of materials in the previous activity on page 75.

**2.** Write the four numbers in each broken diagonal and add them. See the examples in **Figure 10b**:

$$10 + 6 + 7 + 11 = 34$$
$$7 + 13 + 10 + 4 =$$

Find more ways to add broken diagonals.

**3.** Write the four numbers in each 2 × 2 square and add them. One example is:

8 + 13 + 3 + 10 = 34.

There are nine 2 × 2 squares. Find the sum of the four numbers in each square. Is it 34 or a different number?

**4.** There are four 3 × 3 squares. Find the sums of the corner numbers. Here is one example:

13 + 11 + 4 + 6 = 34

**5.** Find the sum of the four corner numbers of the magic square.

**6.** Find other ways to add four numbers to get the sum 34. Here are two ways:

**a.** 1 + 8 + 9 + 16 = 34. Draw lines to connect the numbers to form a parallelogram. Look for other combinations of four numbers that form parallelograms.

**b.** 13 + 2 + 4 + 15 = 34. Draw lines to connect the numbers to form a trapezoid. Look for other combinations of four numbers that form trapezoids. **Figure 11**

Would you agree that this magic square is *PANMAGIC*?

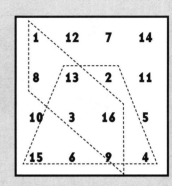

**Panmagic magic square—parallelogram and trapezoid**

**Figure 11**

5

# How People Measure

**W**hen you say that an object is three feet long, are you talking about your actual feet? We use foot as a unit of measure because someone far back in history set the length of this unit and called it a "foot." Before there were standard units that everyone could agree upon, people really did use their fingers, their hands, their arms, and other parts of their bodies as measures. You will learn about the Roman foot and the Egyptian cubit, or arm's length.

In this chapter you will pretend to be a pioneer building a log cabin in Kentucky. Then you will be a member of the Iroquois Confederacy, Native Americans of northeast North America, and your task will be to design a longhouse for the village.

You will make a set of panpipes that you can actually play, perhaps not as well as the masters of the instrument in the high Andes of South America, but well enough to produce a few tunes and have fun.

The last activity in the chapter will bring you right back to the here and now. How can we save the water that is so necessary for life for all the livings things on our planet?

# Standard Measures from Ancient Rome

**H**ave you ever used your hands to show how big something is? Have you used any other part of your body to measure size or distance?

Long before rulers and tape measures were invented, people measured things by using the parts of their bodies. We still use the word *foot* for a certain unit of measure. Is your foot as long as the unit we call a foot?

People living in small villages exchanged goods by barter. Mary would exchange a bowl of eggs for Harry's basketful of apples. Cloth might be measured by the arm's length. But whose arm would be the unit of measure? When Mary buys cloth from Jane, she wants to use her husband's arm as the measuring unit because it is longer than hers. But Jane, who wove the cloth, might want to use her own arm because it is shorter than Mary's.

As trade increased, people realized that they needed to establish standard measures. In the fifteenth and sixteenth centuries, trade was growing among the cities of Italy. The *braccia* (arm's length) became a standard of measure. However, the length of the braccia varied from city to city. A fixed length was necessary to keep peace among buyers and sellers.

The ancient Romans were great builders and engineers. Some of their buildings still stand today, 2,000 years later. The Romans developed the unit of measure called a foot. In their language, called Latin, the word for foot is *pes.* For two or more feet they said *pedes.* The width of the thumb was *uncia.* The English word *inch* comes from *uncia.* Twelve of these units equaled a *pes,* just as twelve inches make a foot.

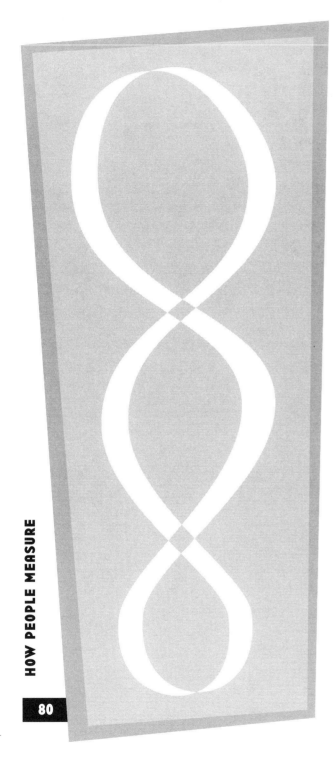

Everyone had to agree on the length of the units called foot and inch. They needed standard measures.

Even when there are standard measures, people will still use parts of their bodies for measuring. When my mother needed to estimate the length of a yard of ribbon, for example, she would hold the spool of ribbon in her right hand and pull out the end of the ribbon along her extended right arm until it reached the tip of her nose. She didn't know that many hundreds of years ago King Edgar of England used that method to set the measure we call a yard.

## MAKE YOUR OWN PERSONAL FOOT RULER

### MATERIALS
- Piece of cardboard or heavy paper, longer than your foot
- Pencil
- Scissors
- Paper

### MAKING THE RULER
**1.** Remove your shoe.

**2.** Trace the outline of your foot on the cardboard.

**3.** Cut out the outline of your foot. This is your personal foot ruler.

## THINGS TO THINK ABOUT AND DO
**1.** Work with a partner. Ask your partner to measure your height using your own foot ruler. Then copy this sentence onto a piece of paper and fill in the blank:

My height is _____ times the length of my foot.

**2.** Use the length of your own foot as a measure. Stand with the back of your heels against the wall. Walk a distance of 10 feet, heel-to-toe. Mark the finishing point with the pencil or other object. Use a standard foot ruler to measure the distance. Write it down. Then ask your friend to do the same. Compare your "personal feet" with your friend's. Which number is larger? What do these numbers tell you about the length of your foot compared with your friend's foot?

**3.** Make a list of English words that are derived from the Latin word for foot or feet; for example, pedal. Can you think of more words that start with ped- and relate to feet?

# Standard Measures from Ancient Egypt

T he ancient Egyptians may have been the first people in the world to adopt standard units of measurement. The Great Pyramid of the pharaoh Khufu, built about 4,600 years ago, was considered one of the Seven Wonders of the Ancient World. The builders needed standard units for its construction. They used a unit called a cubit, the distance from the elbow to the ▮ ▮e middle finger. The "royal c▮ ▮ ▮ in the construction ▮ ▮or everyday

The r
inches
sever
into
wa
it

Math ▮
Math book

## THINGS TO THINK ABOUT AND DO

**1.** Measure your own personal cubit and write the length, to the nearest centimeter. How does it compare with the Egyptian royal cubit? Write a sentence about it.

**2.** How long is the Egyptian palm in centimeters? Measure the width of your palm. How does it compare with the Egyptian palm? Write a sentence about it.

**3.** Make your own personal palm ruler and subdivide it into four equal digits. ▮e the directions for making a per- ▮t ruler, page 80.) Estimate the ▮ of several objects, such as a ▮ (width and length), a pencil, and ▮k in palm units. Write your esti- ▮e. Work with a partner to measure ▮ch object in palm units. Copy and ▮omplete this table:

| | ▮imate (palms) | Measurement (palms) |
| --- | --- | --- |
| | ___ palms | ___ palms |
| | ___ palms | ___ palms |

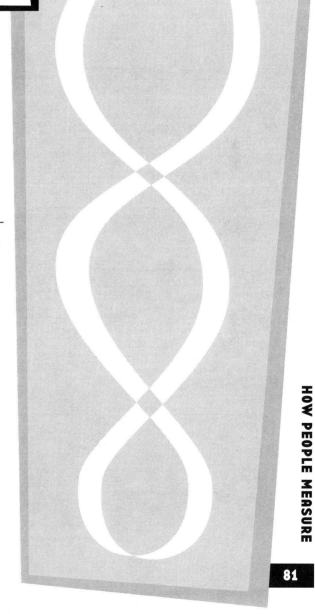

# Log Cabin from the United States

It is the year 1800. Some families came to Kentucky from the state of Virginia. (Kentucky became a state of the United States just eight years before.) The families find forests all around them. They must cut down trees to build their log cabins. They must do all the work themselves and it's not easy.

They decide to build the houses so that each floor is in the shape of a rectangle. They want to make the biggest rectangle they can. They want to cut down as few trees as possible.

Carry out the following experiment to decide the best shape for the floor.

## EXPERIMENT WITH AREA AND PERIMETER

### MATERIALS
- Sheet of heavy paper or cardboard
- Sheet of lined paper
- Ruler
- Pencil
- Scissors

### CARRYING OUT THE EXPERIMENT
**1.** Rule the paper so that you have at least 16 squares, each measuring one inch (2.5 cm) on a side.

**2.** Cut out the 16 squares.

**3.** Arrange the 16 squares in the shape of a rectangle in as many ways as possible. You should find three different ways.

**4.** For each arrangement, note the number of rows, the number of squares in each row, and the distance around in units. Each unit is equal to the length of the side of the square.

**5.** Copy and complete the table below. The first row is done for you. Fill in the second and third rows.

| Rows | Squares in Each Row | Distance Around |
|------|---------------------|-----------------|
| 1    | 16                  | 34 units        |

## THINGS TO THINK ABOUT

**1.** Which rectangle has the smallest distance around? What is the special name for this rectangle?

**2.** What is the perimeter of this rectangle? The perimeter is the distance around it.

**3.** What is the area of this rectangle? The area is the number of squares, called square units.

**4.** Chopping down trees is hard work. The families want to chop as few as possible. What shape should they use for the floors of their homes if they want the largest possible floor space? What else must they think about when they plan the shape of their homes?

**5.** Look at your own home and other buildings in your neighborhood. What is the shape of the floor in most buildings that you see?

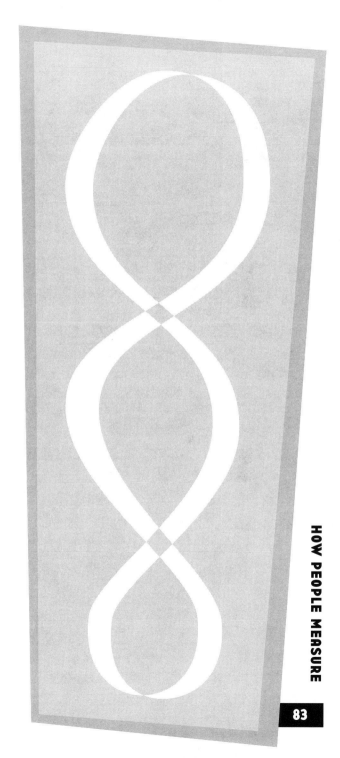

# The Iroquois Longhouse from New York State and Canada

**Iroquois longhouse**

**Figure 1a**

The Iroquois call themselves the *Haudenosaunee*, which means "people of the longhouse." (They are also called the Six Nations of the Iroquois Confederacy.) They live in northern New York State and in southern Ontario and Quebec, but often go to work in other areas. For the past 60 years Iroquois men have climbed far above the ground to construct the tall buildings of New York City. One of the Nations, the Mohawk, is especially noted for its contribution. For example, they were involved in the building of the two 110-story towers of the World Trade Center. When the towers fell on September 11, 2001, about a hundred Mohawk iron workers labored for months at the difficult task of cleaning up after the disaster.

Until about the year 1800, the Haudenosaunee lived in longhouses.

The building, made of saplings and tree bark, was from 110 to 240 feet long and 20 feet high, and housed several related families. Today the longhouse is used mainly for ceremonies.

The construction of a longhouse had to be planned carefully. It had a central hallway running the length of the house. A room for each family led off the hallway. **Figure 1a** (See page 47 for The Calendar of the Iroquois of North America activity.)

## DESIGNING A LONGHOUSE

You have been assigned the task of designing a longhouse for the village. You want to draw several different floor plans. Decide how many rooms you will need. The table below gives some suggestions about the dimensions (length and width) of the longhouse.

| Model | Length | Width | Width of Hallway | Total Area | Total Perimeter |
|-------|--------|-------|------------------|------------|-----------------|
| A | 30 m | 6 m | 1 m | | |
| B | 40 m | 7 m | 1 m | | |

## MATERIALS

- Sheet of lined paper
- Several sheets of ½-inch or centimeter graph paper
- Pencil
- Pen
- Ruler

## DRAWING THE FLOOR PLANS

**1.** Copy the table on lined paper. Complete the table. Find the total area and perimeter of each model. The perimeter is the distance around the longhouse expressed in meters. The total area is the number of square meters enclosed by the perimeter. See the "Log Cabin" Activity on page 82.

**2.** Decide on the scale for drawing the models. Use the same scale for both models. The scale is the number of meters represented by one unit on the graph paper. For example, 1 cm = 3 m.

**3.** Draw each floor plan on a separate sheet of graph paper. Show the subdivisions into rooms. Write the scale. Label all the dimensions on your floor plan, including the size of each room.

## THINGS TO THINK ABOUT AND DO

**1.** What factors did the Haudenosaunee have to take into account when they built their longhouses?

**2.** Research the history of the Six Nations of the Iroquois Confederacy. Where does each nation live today? Where is the main longhouse, the building used for ceremonies?

**3.** Years ago, the storyteller might call the children around him as night fell. Then he would tell tales of talking animals or giants. Look up some of the stories of the Iroquois.

**4.** Design and construct an Iroquois longhouse. Yasmin, a seventh-grade student in New York City, constructed a longhouse using popsicle sticks. **Figure 1b**

**Yasmin's longhouse**

**Figure 1b**

**Bamboo panpipes from Brazil**

---

**Figure 2a**

**Stone panpipes from Peru**

---

**Figure 2b**

# Panpipes from South America

Among the earliest known musical instruments are the panpipes. They are named after the Greek god Pan, the god of shepherds and their flocks. Panpipes are sets of tubes of different lengths, tied together. The player blows across the tops of the pipes to play a tune. The pitch of each tone—how high or how low it is—depends on the length of the pipe. The longer the tube, the lower the pitch of the tone. **Figure 2a**, **Figure 2b**

Panpipes are usually made from hollow wood, such as bamboo. They are especially popular in the Andes mountain region of South America. Several musicians may combine their talents to play a complicated piece of music. One set of panpipes is for the high notes, another plays somewhat lower notes, and another set, which is much larger, plays the very low notes.

You can make your own set of five panpipes and play a tune such as "Mary Had a Little Lamb." They will be tuned to a musical scale. We will call the lowest note C, the next is D,

and so on, up to G. Measure carefully, so that the tones will be correct compared with one another. That means you will have to do some arithmetic.

For the pipe labeled "C" to match the C on the piano or other instrument, it should be 16 cm in length. (You may double each length and make the C-pipe 32 cm long.)

## MATERIALS
- Sheet of paper
- 5 drinking straws
- Ruler in centimeters
- Scissors
- Pencil
- Masking tape or other sticky tape

## MAKING THE PANPIPES

**1.** On your paper make a list along the left side of the page: C, D, E, F, G. Leave some space between the letters to show your calculations.

**2.** The longest straw should measure 16 cm. Call this the C-straw. Cut off the extra piece of the straw. Write the length of the straw next to C.

**3.** The length of the D-straw is ⁸⁄₉ the length of the C-straw. Multiply ⁸⁄₉ by 16 and write your answer, showing your work. The length of the D-straw is:

$$^8/_9 \times 16 = (8 \times 16) \div 9 = 128 \div 9 = 14.2 \text{ cm}$$

**4.** Do the same for the other straws, according to these ratios:

E–length = ⁴⁄₅ × C-length
F–length = ³⁄₄ × C-length
G–length = ²⁄₃ × C-length

**5.** Tape the straws together as in **Figure 3**, arranged from shortest to longest. Keep the uncut ends together and leave a little space between straws. You will blow across them. Wrap tape around all the straws. You may want to place a piece of flattened straw or cardboard under the tape to keep the straws in line.

## THINGS TO THINK ABOUT AND DO

**1.** Play your panpipes. Keep your lips only slightly open and blow across the top of each straw.

**2.** Play "Mary Had a Little Lamb." These are the notes:

E-D-C-D-E-E-E
D-D-D
E-G-G
E-D-C-D-E-E-E
E-D-D-E-D-C

Try other tunes, and make up your own.

**3.** The ancient Greek scientist Pythagoras lived about 2,500 years ago. Historians think he was the first to carry out a scientific experiment—or the first that we know about. He figured out the ratios between the lengths of strings of different pitches on a musical instrument. These are the ratios you used to make your panpipes. Look up Pythagoras in an encyclopedia or on the Web.

**4.** Take several glass tumblers of the same size and shape. Fill each tumbler with a different amount of water. Tap on the edge of the tumbler with a metal spoon. Notice the different pitches. Can you play "Mary Had a Little Lamb" on these glasses? Adjust the amount of water to get the correct pitches.

**5.** Find out why panpipes are named after the Greek god Pan.

**6.** Play a recording of a South American group of musicians playing panpipes. Perhaps you can find one on the Internet.

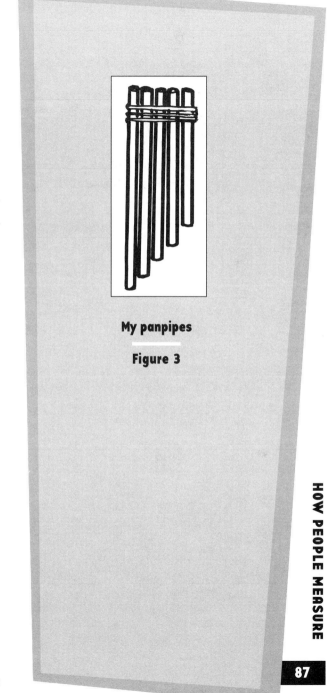

**My panpipes**

**Figure 3**

# Save the Water for the World

**W**e have all the water we need, haven't we? Just turn on the tap, and there it is. But wait a minute! We are using the same water that people had thousands of years ago. Water doesn't grow! In some parts of the world, even in the United States, people don't have the water they need. In many places, people must buy water from big corporations at prices they can't afford. So we must be careful about the water we use.

Does anyone in your family let the tap water run while she or he is not using it? For example, do you turn off the tap while you brush your teeth?

Zena and Chen decided to find out how much water they would save if they turned off the tap while they brushed their teeth. They turned on the tap and counted how many seconds it took to fill an 8-ounce (236 ml) cup with water. It took three seconds. Then they timed how long it took Zena to brush her teeth—two minutes.

## THINGS TO FIGURE OUT

**1.** How much water was running if the tap was on while Zena brushed her teeth? You may want to use a calculator. Write down how you worked out the answer.

**2.** Zena needed only one cup of water to brush her teeth. How much water was wasted by leaving the tap on?

**3.** Zena brushes her teeth twice a day. How much water does she waste by leaving the tap running every day? In one week? In one year?

You may check your answers on page 154.

## THINGS TO THINK ABOUT AND DO

**1.** Think about how you and your family use water. Can you find ways to save water, for instance, when washing dishes or taking a shower?

**2.** What other types of things should we save? Does your community have a policy about recycling? What items are recycled? How is it done? What happens to the garbage in your community?

**3.** Is there a group in your school or your neighborhood that works on recycling? Find out.

**4.** Read the book *The Black Snowman*, by Philip Mendez. In this story, a boy learns about his African heritage as he recycles cans and bottles to earn money for a gift for his mother.

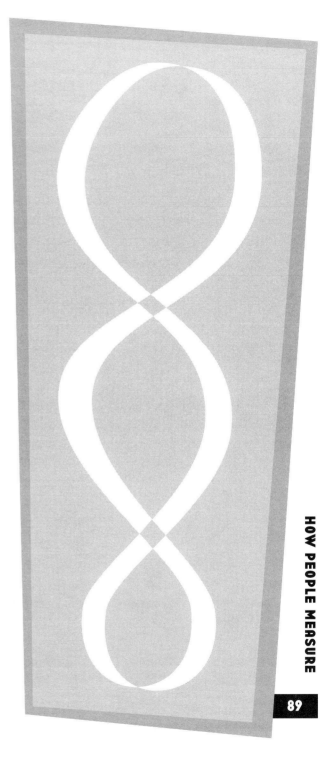

## 6

# Puzzles with Dots, String, and Paper Strips

**P**eople in different parts of the world have used sets of dots to help them draw designs. Very often they drew these designs in the sand or the soil. Of course such drawings didn't last long. Boys in parts of West Africa play a game called *Julirde* that starts with a square of dots. The challenge is to draw a diagram that has certain features. Children in Angola, farther south in Africa, learned their lessons by listening to stories. As the storyteller, a respected older man, recited his tale, he drew pictures, called *sona*, around a grid of dots to illustrate the story. In southern India, girls learn from their mothers the skill of drawing *kolam* designs on the ground at the threshold of their home to greet visitors. These designs start with a grid of dots.

The string and bead puzzle, popular in both China and Africa, presents a real challenge. At first I had trouble doing it myself, so I have tried to make the directions very clear. Once you have mastered the puzzle, you can amaze your friends with your skill.

A different trick that will astound your friends makes use of a certain kind of paper loop called a Möbius strip. You will be surprised at the results when you cut the strip in certain ways. This trick is from Germany.

Look for all of these regions and countries on a map.

# Julirde from West Africa

*J*ulirde, or the "game of the mosque," is played by boys of the Fulbe ethnic group in West Africa. The Fulbe are mainly cattle herders. They move from place to place looking for feed for their animals. They live in a region that extends from Senegal to Cameroon. Boys help with the cattle while girls have other tasks. This game keeps the boys on their toes and helps them pass the time while the cattle are grazing.

The Fulbe people, also called Fulani in English, have a history going back many centuries. Their ancestors were rulers of several African kingdoms. In the eleventh century many Fulbe converted to the religion of Islam. The word *Islam* means "peace." The mosque is the place of prayer for followers of Islam. That explains the name of the game.

Here are the rules of the game as played by the Fulbe boys. They drew their game board in the sand or soil. You may use paper and pencil or a geoboard.

## RULES OF THE JULIRDE GAME

**1.** Draw a set of dots to form a nine by nine square. **Figure 1**

**2.** Draw a closed loop that connects all the dots. You may not retrace a line segment. The loop must go from one dot to another dot in the same row or column. Diagonal lines are not allowed. The loop ends at the starting point.

**3.** There must be an opening on each of the four sides of the square for people to enter the mosque. The letter E marks each opening in **Figure 2.**

**4.** If the side of the square has an odd number of dots, the middle dot is not in the game.

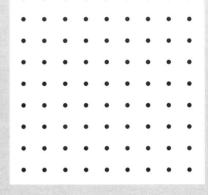

**9 × 9 square grid of dots**

**Figure 1**

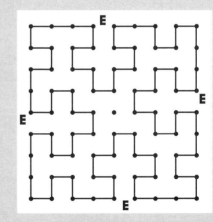

**Julirde on a 9 × 9 grid, with turn symmetry**

**Figure 2**

Source: Paulus Gerdes, "Exploring the Game of Julirde," *Teaching Children Mathematics.*

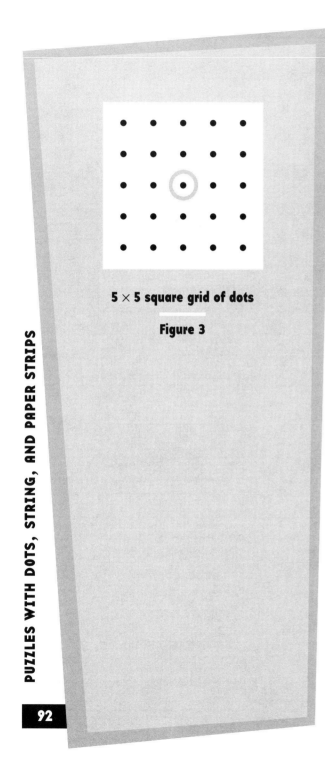

**5 × 5 square grid of dots**

**Figure 3**

**5.** The game drawing must be symmetrical; that is, it looks the same from all four sides of the square.

The Julirde in **Figure 2** seems complicated, doesn't it? Don't worry—you will start with simpler versions. Here are some things to look for:

- The loop is closed; it came back to the starting point.
- The loop went through every point except the center point.
- The connecting line either went straight ahead or made a 90° turn.
- No line segment was retraced.
- There is at least one opening on each of the four sides of the mosque.
- The diagram looks the same from all four sides of the square. It has turn symmetry. To check, rotate the page a quarter turn, then another and another, until you are back to the starting position. Notice how every side of the square looks the same.

Let's start with an easier version of the Julirde game.

## MATERIALS
- Dot paper. You can buy this at craft or school supply stores. If you don't have any, use graph paper or lined paper.
- Pencil
- Eraser

## PLAYING JULIRDE
**1.** Draw a 5 × 5 square of dots. Use dot paper, if possible. Otherwise draw the dots on graph paper or lined paper.

**2.** Draw a small circle around the center dot. That dot is not in the game. **Figure 3**

**3.** Draw a closed loop that connects all the dots and leaves an opening on each of four sides.

**4.** Is your drawing symmetrical—does it look the same from all four sides?

It may take some practice before you get it right. That's how you learn what works and what doesn't. Don't give up!

## THINGS TO THINK ABOUT AND DO

**1.** Try to make a Julirde drawing on a 3 × 3 square of dots. Then try a 4 × 4 square. Can you make a drawing that has openings on all four sides? Can you make a drawing that has openings on just two opposite sides?

**2.** Make a drawing on a 5 × 5 square that is different from the one you already made.

**3.** Make a Julirde drawing on a 6 × 6 square. You may find that it does not look the same from all four sides. What type of symmetry does it have? If you fold the diagram down the center, does one half match the other half? This is called *line symmetry*. If your drawing does not have any symmetry, try again. **Figure 4**

**4.** Experiment with square grids of different sizes: 7 × 7, 8 × 8, 9 × 9, etc. Are they symmetrical? What type of symmetry do they have?

**5.** In general, which drawings have turn symmetry? Which have line symmetry?

**6.** Play the game with a friend.

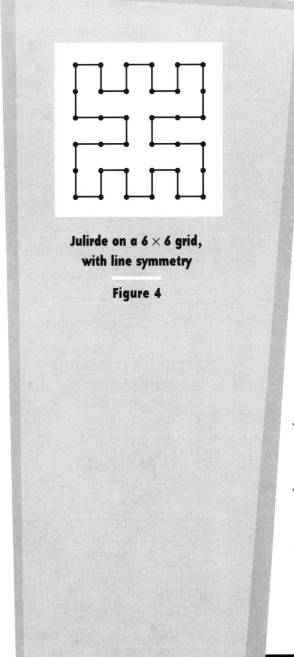

**Julirde on a 6 × 6 grid, with line symmetry**

**Figure 4**

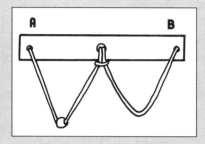

**Bead and string puzzle**

**Figure 5**

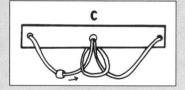

**Figure 6a**

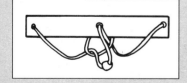

**Figure 6b**

# Bead and String Puzzle from China and West Africa

The author Wei Zhang collected puzzles from China, her home-land, as well as from other places (see the Bibliography on page 156). This puzzle, and others like it, have a long history in both China and West Africa. The trick is to pass the bead or ring from one side of the string to the other. The center hole is too small for the bead to pass through. How can it be done?

In China people made the puzzle from wire or string. They used old Chinese coins, which had a hole in the middle. Wealthier people had puzzles of ivory bars and beads.

In rural areas of West Africa, the materials were a twig of a tree and vines woven into a cord. People made beads of clay and bored holes through them.

You can make your own puzzle. **Figure 5**

## MATERIALS
- Heavy cardboard or poster board, about 2 inches x 10 inches (5 cm X 25 cm)
- About 30 inches (75 cm) of thick string
- Ruler
- Scissors or sharp knife
- Large bead or ring

## MAKING THE PUZZLE
**1.** Make three holes in the cardboard, as in the diagram. The center hole should be large enough for four strands to go through. If you use a knife, make sure a grown-up is with you to help.

**2.** Find the center of the string. Push the doubled-up end through the center hole from front to back to make a loop.

**3.** Push the loose ends of the string through the loop.

**4.** Place a bead on one end of the string, and thread the string through the hole marked A.

**5.** Tie the string at hole A. You may want to put a bow in it so that you can untie it if the string gets tangled.

**6.** Tie the other end of the string at hole B.

## SOLVING THE PUZZLE
**Figures 6a, b, c, d, e, f**

**1.** Pull the loop at C forward, as in **Figure 6a**.

**2.** Pass the bead through the loop, as in **Figure 6b**.

**3.** The strands are crossed in the back of the puzzle board. Pull the string through the hole at C, from back to front, so that the four strands come through the hole, forming two loops, as in **Figure 6c**. Put your finger through the two loops.

**4.** Pass the bead through the two loops, from left to right, as in **Figure 6d**.

**5.** Put your hand in back of the puzzle and pull the string crossing back through hole C.

**6.** Follow the strand from hole B. Pull the bead through the loop from left to right, as in **Figure 6e**.

**7.** The bead is on the strand from hole B, as in **Figure 6f**. You have solved the puzzle!

## THINGS TO THINK ABOUT AND DO
**1.** Try to transfer the bead from the right side to the left side of the puzzle board without reading the directions. You may look at the diagrams, if necessary.

**2.** Figure out what is happening to the knots in the string while you are solving the puzzle.

**3.** Demonstrate this puzzle to a group of friends. Challenge them to transfer the bead to the other side of the puzzle board.

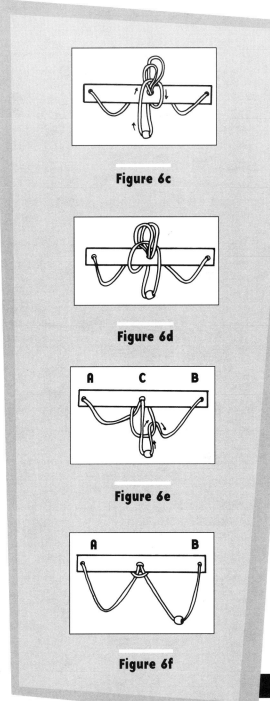

Figure 6c

Figure 6d

Figure 6e

Figure 6f

# Möbius Strip Surprises from Germany

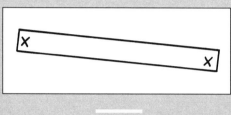

**Figure 7**

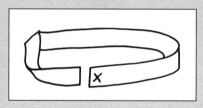

**Figure 8**

**H**ere is a puzzle that you can use to surprise your friends. All you have to do is cut a strip of paper a certain way. Try it and then read why it works. (Answers on page 154.)

## MATERIALS

- Several strips of paper, about 2 inches by 20 inches (5 cm X 50 cm). If you don't have long strips, cut a sheet of 8½-by-11-inch paper into four long strips and glue two pieces end to end to make a longer strip.
- Pencil
- Glue or sticky tape
- Scissors

## MAKING THE MÖBIUS STRIP

**1.** Take one long strip. Mark an X at each end on the same side of the paper. **Figure 7**

**2.** Hold one end in each hand. Twist one end and place one end over the other end so that the two X-marks show. This is called a half-twist. **Figure 8**

**3.** Glue the ends together to form a closed band. A closed band with a half-twist is called a Möbius strip.

## CUTTING THE MÖBIUS STRIP— FIRST EXPERIMENT

**1.** Draw a line down the center of the strip until you reach your starting point.

**2.** Guess what the outcome will be when you cut along the line.

**3.** Cut along the line.

**4.** Describe the outcome. Were you surprised by it?

## CUTTING THE MÖBIUS STRIP— SECOND EXPERIMENT

**1.** Make another Möbius strip, a loop with a half twist.

**2.** Draw a line about one third of the way from the right edge until you come back to the starting point.

**3.** Guess what the outcome will be when you cut along the line.

**4.** Cut along the line.

**5.** Describe the outcome.

A German mathematician, August Möbius, discovered this amazing strip about 150 years ago. Isn't it surprising that no one had known about it until then? But once it was known, it was used to good advantage. Conveyor belts in factories—the moving belts that carry materials from place to place—were made in the shape of Möbius bands. They lasted twice as long as the usual belts because they had only one side!

Artists have had fun with Möbius strips. M. C. Escher loved to draw impossible situations, such as staircases that never end. In one of his paintings he has a line of ants crawling along a Möbius strip.

Here is a Möbius strip poem:

A mathematician confided

That a Möbius band is one-sided;

But you'll get quite a laugh,

If you cut one in half,

For it stays in one piece when divided.

## THINGS TO THINK ABOUT AND DO

**1.** Show that a Möbius strip has only one side. Draw a red X at one end of the strip and a black X at the other end, on the same side. Twist one end. Place one end over the other so that both X's show. Glue the ends together; be sure that the two X marks show. Now start with the red X and run your finger along the band until you come back to the red X. Don't lift your finger. Did you pass the black X along the way?

**2.** Carry out this experiment. Cut a Möbius strip one quarter of the way from the edge. What is the result?

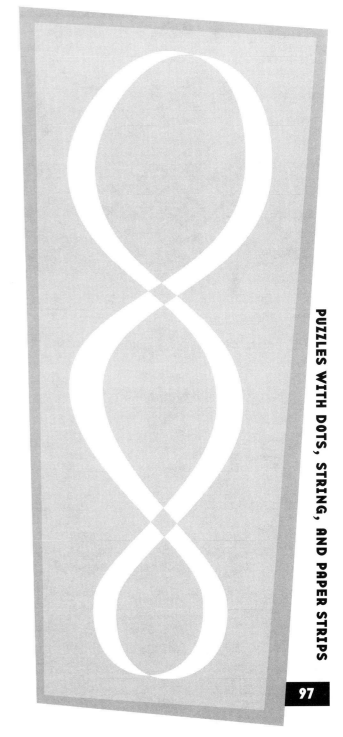

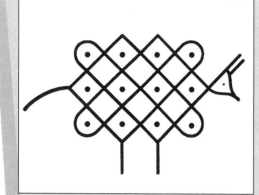

**Antelope on a 3 × 4 grid of dots**

**Figure 9a**

Source: Paulus Gerdes, *Desenhos da Africa*

# Sand Drawings I: Animal Pictures from Angola, Africa

Imagine that there are no schools of the kind you attend. How do children learn? Who teaches them? Before most children went to school, they were taught by their parents and by the older people of their society.

The Chokwe people live in northeastern Angola, a country in southwestern Africa. They are mainly farmers, but they also hunt animals for food. Before the days of radio and television, before the time of schools, children would gather around an old person in the evening, after the work was done. They would sit around a campfire or under the shade of a tree and learn about their history, how to get along with people, and how animals behaved.

The Chokwe people are known for their wonderful art. They decorate the walls of their homes with interesting designs. When the elder tells a story, he draws a picture in the soil to make the story come alive. First he makes a grid of dots, then he traces a design between the dots while telling the story. These designs are called *sona*; one design is a *lusona*. Usually he draws the lusona without taking his finger off the soil or pausing in the storytelling.

Today we will talk about and draw two animals: an antelope, and the path of a wild chicken as it is chased by a hunter.

## MATERIALS

- Several sheets of graph paper (use lined paper if you don't have graph paper)
- Pencil
- Eraser
- Colored pens
- Ruler or straightedge

## DRAWING THE ANTELOPE

**Figure 9a**

**1.** On the graph paper draw a 3 × 4 grid of dots to form a rectangle. Hold the paper so that the lines run diagonally.

**2.** With your pencil, start the drawing on the left side, between the 2nd and 3rd row. Draw your lines through the intersections of the graph paper lines, the points where the lines cross. You may want to use a ruler to draw straight lines. **Figure 9b**

**3.** Continue to draw the body of the antelope without lifting your pencil off the paper. Draw each line until it reaches the turning point, just past the last dot in the row or column. **Figure 9c**

**4.** Add the head, legs, and tail to the body.

**5.** Go over the lines with a colored pen.

Does your antelope look like **Figure 9a**?

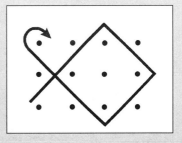

**Figure 9b**

**Body of the antelope**

**Figure 9c**

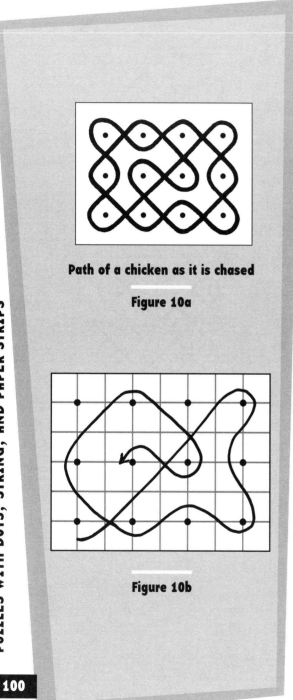

**Path of a chicken as it is chased**

**Figure 10a**

**Figure 10b**

## DRAWING THE PATH OF THE CHICKEN

Look at the path of the chicken as the hunter is chasing it. It makes some sharp turns, almost retracing its path. **Figure 10a**

**1.** Draw a 4 × 3 grid of points on graph paper. Skip an intersection between each pair of dots.

**2.** With your pencil start drawing in the lower left and continue as in **Figure 10b**. Try to do the whole drawing without taking your pencil off the paper. **Figure 10b**

**3.** Complete the path of the chicken. It finally comes back to the starting point.

**4.** Go over the drawing with a colored pen. Does it look like **Figure 10a**?

## THINGS TO THINK ABOUT

**1.** Look at the drawing of the body of the antelope in **Figure 9c**. Does it have a line of symmetry? Can you fold the paper on a line so that one half fits over the other half of the drawing? How many different lines of symmetry can you find? Can you rotate (turn) the paper so that the drawing will look the same in a different position? In how many different positions does the drawing look the same?

**2.** Look at the drawing of the chased chicken. Does it have line symmetry? Does it have turn symmetry?

You may find answers on page 154.

## WHAT ELSE CAN YOU DO? Figure 11

Here is another drawing of the path of a chicken as it is hunted down. This chicken led the hunter on a merry chase!

Take a thin sheet of paper and lay it over the diagram. Fasten it down with paper clips so that it doesn't move. Then try to trace the whole drawing without lifting your pencil off the paper. You may start any place, and you should end at the starting point.

After you have traced the diagram, try to draw it on a 6 × 5 grid of points.

Dr. Paulus Gerdes is a mathematician living in Mozambique. Both his country and Angola are former colonies of Portugal, as is Brazil, in South America. Dr. Gerdes has written several books about the *sona* of Angola. One book, published in Brazil, is for children (see the Bibliography on page 157). It is in Portuguese, the language spoken in Brazil. I hope the book will be translated into English.

**Path of a chicken as it is chased**

**Figure 11**

# Sand Drawings II: The Story of Three Villages from Angola

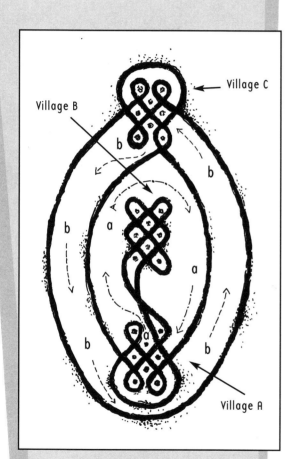

**Figure 12**

Source: Th. Centner, *L'enfant Africain et ses Jeux*

**H**ere is another tale told by the Chokwe elders. It is in a collection of African games by a Frenchwoman named Theodora Centner. By the time she wrote about them, the practice was dying out, and very few people still knew how to draw the pictures and tell the stories.

**Figure 12**

The drawing shows three villages, labeled A, B, and C.

The people of Village A were really upset with Village C. They sent a child (a) to tell the people of Village C: "You had better take care of your goats. They are eating all our corn! If this doesn't stop we are going to have to fight you!"

The boy set out, but he missed the entrance to Village C. Without knowing it, he had returned to his own village. He yelled: "Take better care of your goats!"

His parents scolded him: "We send you to Village C, and here you end up back home." People in the village made fun of the boy.

Several days later the people of Village C sent a messenger (b) to invite all the hunters of the neighboring villages to a big bush fire. The boy left Village C and walked for a long time. He passed right by the other villages without seeing them, and came back to his parents' house. Unable to get into the house, he retraced his steps and came home very late. He had also failed to carry out the errand.

## THINGS TO THINK ABOUT AND DO

**1.** Why do you think both boys failed to carry out their tasks? What lesson does this story teach young children?

**2.** With your finger or a pencil tip, trace the path of the boy (a) from Village A and the path of the boy (b) from Village C. Follow the direction of the arrows.

**3.** Lay a sheet of thin paper over the diagram of the three villages and fasten it with paper clips. Trace the whole drawing with a pencil. Can it be done in one sweep, without lifting your pencil off the paper?

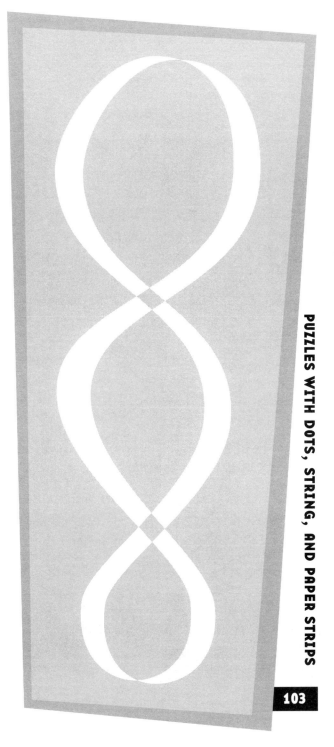

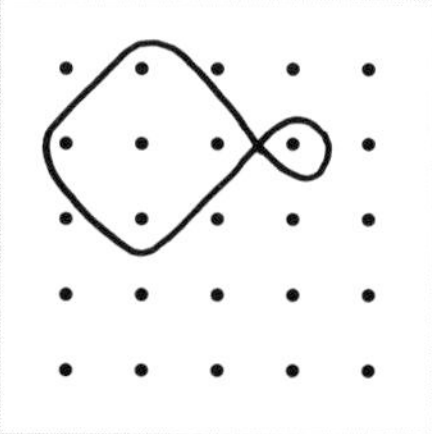

**Figure 13a**

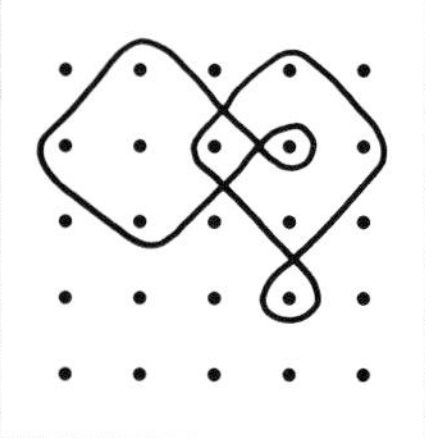

**Figure 13b**

**Figure 13c**

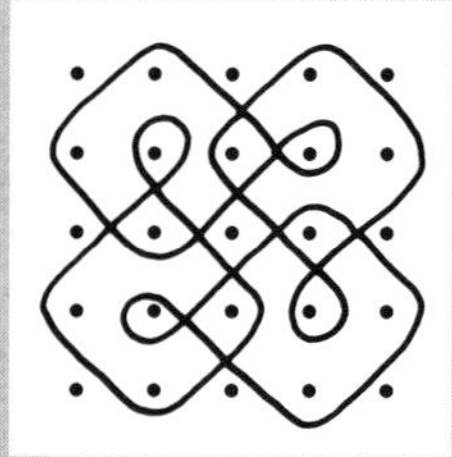

**Figure 13d**

# Sand Drawings III: Welcome to Our Home *from India*

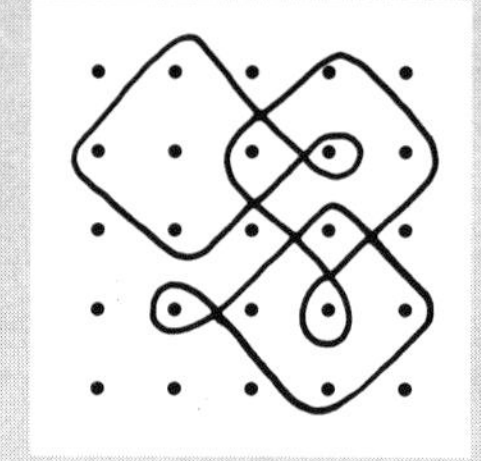

**D**ahti lives in southern India. She is learning from her mother how to draw figures in the sand. Every morning her mother sweeps the threshold (entrance) to her house. Then she spreads a mixture of water and cow dung over the area. She takes a handful of rice powder and carefully sprinkles it over the area to create beautiful designs. Ants and other insects will eat some of the rice powder. The remainder is swept away.

Women in the state of Tamil Nadu, in southeastern India, have been making these *kolam* designs for centuries. It is a way of welcoming visitors to their homes. Today they may use other types of white powder or chalk to make the designs.

Usually they start with a grid of dots. The design may connect the dots, or go around them. Often the design is a continuous figure, drawn without stopping until it ends at the beginning, like the cycle of life and death.

Dahti's mother is showing her how to make a simple figure. You can make the same figure with pencil and paper.

## MATERIALS
- Dot paper or graph paper
- Pencil
- Eraser
- Colored pens

## DRAWING THE DESIGN
### Figure 13a, b, c, d

**1.** Mark off a 5 × 5 square of dots on dot paper, or draw the dots on graph paper.

**2.** Draw the design in **Figure 13a** with your pencil. Go over it with a colored pen.

**3.** Turn the paper a quarter turn, or 90°. Repeat the same design in pencil, as in **Figure 13b**. Use a pen of a different color to go over the line.

**4.** Turn the paper 90° again. Draw the design and go over it with a colored pen. **Figure 13c**

**5.** Turn the paper 90° and repeat the design again, as in **Figure 13d**. Color it.

**6.** Finish the border with a line curving in and out between the dots along the edge of the design. **Figure 13e**

### THINGS TO THINK ABOUT AND DO

**1.** Let's look at the symmetry of the kolam design you just made. Does it look the same as you rotate the paper? Think about how you drew the design. In how many different positions does the design look the same?

**2.** Does the design have line symmetry?

**3.** Discuss with your friends the custom of drawing kolam designs.

**4.** According to the author Marcia Ascher (see Bibliography on page 155), computer scientists are using kolam designs to set up rules for drawing computer pictures and creating new kinds of computer languages. Look at the design in **Figure 14**, "Anklets of Krishna." The diagram, based on Ascher's book, shows several stages in drawing the kolam design. What instructions would a person at a computer need to draw the design?

**Kolam design**

**Figure 13e**

Marcia Ascher, *Mathematics Elsewhere*, Princeton University Press, 2002

**Anklets of Krishna**

**Figure 14**

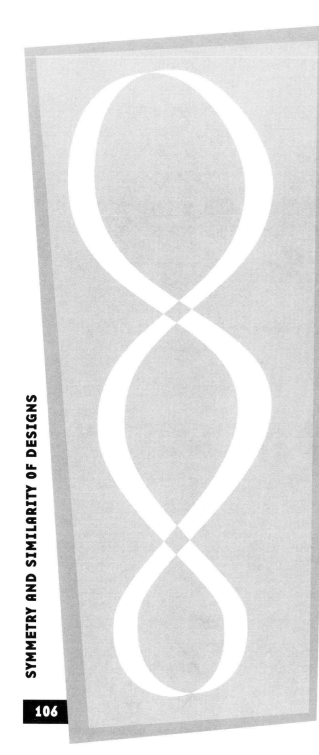

# 7

# Symmetry and Similarity of Designs

**W**hat is the meaning of the word *symmetry*? Your body has symmetry. The left half of you matches the right half of you. Your face has symmetry—the left eye matches the right eye, the left nostril matches the right nostril, maybe not exactly, but pretty nearly.

The word *symmetry* comes from the Greek words that mean "same measure." We will discuss two kinds of symmetry: line symmetry and turn symmetry.

Let's first talk about *line symmetry*. The doll in **Figure 5a** (page 114) has line symmetry, just as your body has. Imagine a line drawn down the center of the doll. If you fold the photo on this line, the left side and the right side of the doll match. You can also place a mirror on this line. The half of the doll that you see in the mirror is just like the half behind the mirror. This imaginary line is called an *axis of symmetry*.

What is *turn symmetry*? Look at the five-pointed star, like the stars in the flag of the United States. Rotate the page. The star looks the same in five different positions as you turn the book. Another name for turn symmetry is *rotational symmetry*. The star also has five different *lines* of symmetry. **Figure 1a**

*Similarity* deals with the size of an object. Two objects that have the same shape but different size are *similar.* The two stars are similar. They have the same shape, but one is larger than the other. **Figure 1b**

In this chapter you will learn about the beautiful designs on Native American beadwork, buffalo skin carrying cases, rugs, and quilts. The symmetrical doll is from the culture of the Asante people of Ghana, in West Africa. Then you will learn about flags of many countries, especially the flags that have stars. Stars are also the design element in many patchwork quilts. How many ways can you make a star design using squares and triangles? You will try several different ways.

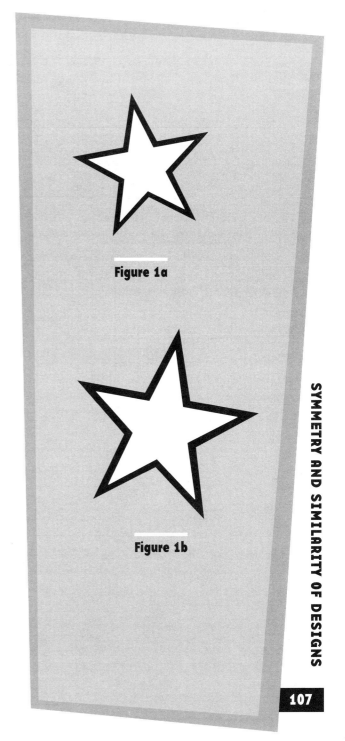

Figure 1a

Figure 1b

# Native American Beadwork–Part I

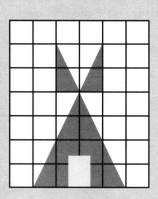

**Tipi pattern**

**Figure 1c**

**E**uropeans gave the name East-ern *Sioux* (SOO) to the Dakota people. Dakota means "society of friends," people working together. They lived in the Great Plains. Later, two states were named after them: North Dakota and South Dakota. The Western Sioux called themselves Lakota. By the early eighteenth century the Sioux were roaming the plains on horseback to hunt buffalo. Buffalo meat was their main food. Buffalo skins were used to make clothing, bags, the tipis in which they lived, and many other objects. These objects were often decorated with beadwork or painting.

Native peoples used several different types of materials to make beads: shells, bones, claws, stones, and minerals. The shell beads of the East Coast peoples were later used as money, called *wampum* (see page 53). Early beads were called pony beads. By the mid-1800s they used smaller beads for sewn beadwork decorations.

## MAKING A BEADWORK TIPI DECORATION

Josie is planning to decorate her jacket with beadwork in the style of the Dakota people. She finds a pattern for making a tipi decoration. Now she must figure out how many beads she will need. **Figure 1c**

Her friend Eddie likes the tipi pattern. He wants to decorate his jacket with beadwork, too, but his tipi will be twice as wide and twice as high as the tipi in the grid pattern.

## MATERIALS

- Grid paper
- Pencil
- Ruler
- Colored pencils or markers

## PLANNING TO MAKE THE TIPI

**1.** Count the number of grid squares in the design. How will you count the partial squares? You can use the idea of symmetry to help you figure it out.

**2.** Copy the design on your grid paper. Color the tipi.

**3.** About 10 beads will cover one small square. How many beads will Josie need for the pattern?

**4.** Draw Eddie's tipi on the same grid. First outline it lightly in pencil. Be sure that it is two times as wide and two times as high as Josie's. Color the design. Eddie's design is similar to Josie's. It is the same shape but a different size.

**5.** Count the small squares in Eddie's design. Figure out how many beads he will need.

**6.** Eddie's tipi design requires _____ times as many beads as Josie's. What number goes in the blank space?

You may check your answers on page 154.

## THINGS TO THINK ABOUT AND DO

**1.** Suppose you wanted to make a tipi design similar to the one in **Figure 1c** but three times as wide and three times as high? How many beads do you think you will need?

**2.** Draw this tipi on graph paper and color it. Make sure that it is 12 spaces wide and 18 spaces high. Figure out how many beads you will need by counting the small squares and multiplying that number by ten. Does your answer agree with the answer in the previous question?

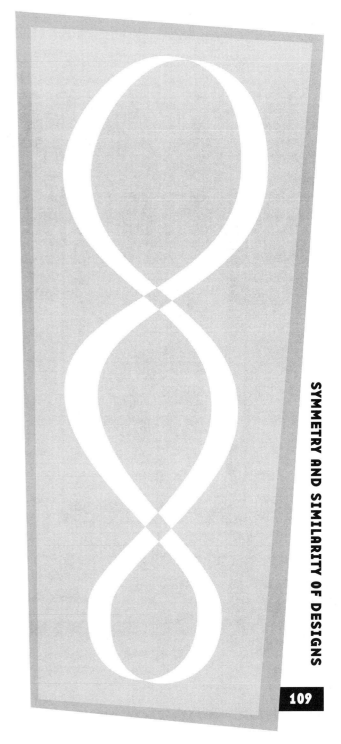

# Native American Beadwork–Part II

**Menominee medicine bag**

**Figure 2a**

Source: Le Roy H. Appleton, *American Indian Design and Decoration*

The Native people of North America made beautiful beadwork designs on clothing, bags, and other items. Different nations developed their own styles. People in the Great Lakes region often made flower designs. The design in **Figure 2a** is on a Menominee medicine bag. Count the petals on the large flower. What else do you see in the design? Does the design have symmetry? What pattern do you see in the borders?

A young girl might learn to do beadwork with a simple flower design, like the one on the grid. Examine the grid. Each space measures ½ centimeter. Each small square is ¼ of a square centimeter. The flower has eight petals. About 30 beads can cover one square centimeter. **Figure 2b**

## MATERIALS
- Grid paper
- Pencil
- Ruler
- Colored pencils or markers

## MAKING A BEADWORK FLOWER DECORATION

**1.** Count the number of squares covered by the flower. Use the symmetry of the design to make counting as simple as possible. Remember that each square on the paper measures ¼ square centimeter. How many square centimeters are covered by the flower?

**2.** Copy the flower on your grid paper and color it.

**3.** About how many beads does the design require? Work it out, then check your answer on page 154.

**4.** Suppose you want to make a design that was similar to this one but larger. You want the flower to have the same shape, but each part should have twice the length and twice the width of the original design. How many square centimeters will it cover on the grid paper? About how many beads will you need?

**5.** Draw this design on grid paper. Check your answers to the previous question. Were they correct?

## THINGS TO THINK ABOUT AND DO

**1.** Find examples of Native American beadwork. Do you notice that different peoples had different styles?

**2.** Look for instructions about doing beadwork and try it yourself.

**3.** The ancient Egyptians, 4,000 years ago, first made sketches on a grid before drawing larger designs on temple walls. Then the artist drew a larger grid on the wall. In this way the artist was able to keep the correct proportions in the figures. Look for pictures of paintings on Egyptian temple walls.

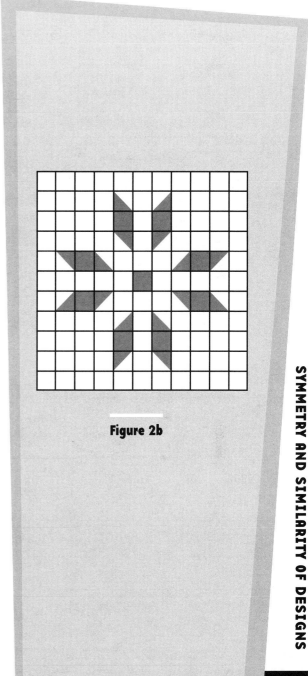

**Figure 2b**

# Native American Painted Designs

**Design on a Dakota rawhide bag**

**Figure 3a**

Source: LeRoy H. Appleton, *American Indian Design and Decoration*

The Arapaho, Lakota, Dakota, and many other native peoples moved to the plains and prairies of the Midwest after 1700. With so many different language groups coming together, they developed a very useful sign language. When the Spanish introduced the horse to the area, these people suddenly had transportation. They abandoned their farms and villages and became nomads. They hunted buffalo, deer, and other animals. The buffalo was the mainstay of their lives, and they used almost every bit of the animal for various purposes.

As Europeans moved across the prairies, killing the buffalo and setting up their own communities, the Native Americans were forced to give up the nomadic way of life. Today some live on reservations, while others have moved to cities and towns.

The Native Americans used dyes made from berries, roots, and other parts of plants to paint designs on buffalo skins. The two designs shown here are similar to the decorations they painted on many objects. The Dakota and Arapaho designs appeared on their rawhide buffalo skin bags. **Figure 3a**, **Figure 3b**

Examine the two designs. Name the different shapes that make up each design. Notice the symmetry of each design. If you fold the design on a vertical line drawn down the middle, the left side of the main part of the design fits over the right side. Which sections of the design break up the symmetry?

You can copy one or both designs, making your design large enough to cover a *parfleche*, a Plains Indian carrying case. Your design will be similar to that in the illustration; it will have the same shape, but a different size.

## MATERIALS

- Plain paper
- Pencil
- Eraser
- Ruler
- Crayons, markers, or paint

## MAKING A NATIVE AMERICAN PAINTED DESIGN

**1.** Choose one of the designs to copy. You may decide to copy just part of the design.

**2.** Measure the design in the illustration and write down the width and length.

**3.** You may want the width and length of your design to be twice that of the original (or three times as large). Write down the width and length of your design.

**4.** Use your pencil and ruler to sketch the outline of your design on your paper.

**5.** Decide how you will complete the remainder of the design, and sketch it in pencil. Keep the proportions the same as in the original. Your design is similar to the design in **Figure 3a** or **3b**.

**6.** Color your design.

## THINGS TO THINK ABOUT AND DO

**1.** The Lakota and other tribes kept a record of their history by painting symbols of events on buffalo hide. The year-by-year record was called the Winter Count. A well-known record covered the period from 1801 to 1870. Find information about the Winter Count. You may want to make a daily or weekly record in pictures of your own life.

**2.** Find other Native American designs that you would like to copy. You can use designs that are the same size as in the illustrations or enlarged, but keep the same proportions.

**Design on an Arapaho rawhide bag**

### Figure 3b

Source: LeRoy H. Appleton, *American Indian Design and Decoration*

# Akua ba Doll from Ghana

**Gold weight in the form of an Oware board**

---

**Figure 4**

**Asante akua ba**

---

**Figure 5a**

Source: Private collection of Mr. and Mrs. M. Abelson

The Asante (also called Ashanti) people of Ghana, West Africa, have long been known as artists in metal, wood, and textiles. They created the famous kente cloth that has become popular in the United States. For centuries they were involved in the gold trade. Traders kept sets of brass weights for measuring gold dust. These were not ordinary weights. Some represented people at work, others were in the form of animals and birds, while still others had geometric patterns. **Figure 4** is a tiny board for the Oware game, the version of Mankala popular among the Asante. It is about four centimeters long.

The Asante played Oware on beautiful carved wooden boards that were passed down through generations of a family. Artists also created many types of carved wooden stools, each having a special function. Some were reserved for the king.

**Figure 5a** is a wooden figure called *akua ba* in the language of the Asante. People may call it a doll, but it is not a toy. A woman who is about to give birth to a child wears the akua ba in the back of her wraparound waistcloth. The purpose is to have a safe birth and a healthy child. The akua ba is called a fertility doll.

Examine the picture of the akua ba. What is the shape of the head? What features do you see on the face? What about arms and legs? Are the proportions of the parts of the body like those of a real child? Does the doll have symmetry?

## MAKING AN *AKUA BA*

### MATERIALS
- Plain paper
- Cardboard
- Pencil
- Ruler
- Compass or jar lid (or other circular object)
- Brown and black crayons or markers

**1.** Decide how large you want to make your akua ba. You might want it to be two or three times as tall as the picture in **Figure 5a**. Your doll will be taller by a factor of two or three.

**2.** Measure the parts of the doll's body—the diameter of the head; the length of the neck, the arm, and the body; and any other measurements you will need. Write them down.

**3.** Multiply each measurement by the factor you decided upon.

**4.** Draw the doll lightly in pencil on the cardboard. Use a compass or jar lid to draw the head. Draw the features on the face and any other details you see.

**5.** Go over the features and other details with the black crayon. Make them as dark as possible, so that they will show after you have colored the whole doll.

**6.** Color the doll with the brown crayon.

**7.** Cut out your akua ba.

### THINGS TO THINK ABOUT AND DO
**1.** The Fanti people of Ghana carve fertility dolls similar to the illustration **Figure 5b**. How is the shape of this doll different from the akua ba you made? You might make a doll similar to the Fanti fertility doll.

**2.** Find pictures of Asante wooden stools and Oware boards.

**Fanti fertility doll**

**Figure 5b**

Source: Geoffrey Williams, *African Designs*

**Figure 6a**

**Figure 6b**

**Figure 6c**

# Our Alphabet from Ancient Rome

The alphabet we use was invented by the Romans more than 2,000 years ago. The same alphabet is used for many European and other languages.

## SYMMETRY OF THE ALPHABET

Some letters of the alphabet have several types of symmetry. Some have no symmetry at all. You can analyze the letters for symmetry.

**1.** Write the alphabet in plain capital letters, with no fancy doodads or decorations.

**2.** Imagine that you have a cutout of the letter E. Flip it upside down over an imaginary horizontal line through the middle. The letter E looks just the same as in the original position.

Make a list of all the letters of the alphabet that have this type of line symmetry. **Figure 6a**

**3.** Imagine that you have a cutout of the letter A. Flip it over an imaginary vertical line through the middle so that the point stays at the top. The letter looks exactly the same as in the original position. List all the letters of the alphabet that have this kind of line symmetry. **Figure 6b**

**4.** Imagine that you have a cutout of the letter S. Give it a half turn. The letter S looks just about the same as in the original position. List the letters of the alphabet that have this type of turn symmetry. **Figure 6c**

**5.** Some letters have more than one type of symmetry. Make a list of these letters.

**6.** Compare your lists. Which letters appear on two lists? On three lists?

## THINGS TO THINK ABOUT AND DO

**1.** Did you find any letters that have exactly two types of symmetry? There are none! Why not?

**2.** Some words, written in capital letters, look the same when they are flipped over.

**a.** Make a list of words that look the same when they are flipped over a horizontal line. Look at your list of letters with that type of symmetry to help you think of words.

**b.** Make a list of words that look the same when they are flipped over a vertical line.

**c.** Write words that look the same when you give the paper a half turn.

**3.** Can you find words that can be flipped over or turned to make different words?

**4.** The Greek, Hebrew, and Arabic languages have their own alphabets. In fact, the Romans got some of their letters from the Greeks. Look up the history of alphabets. **Figure 6d**

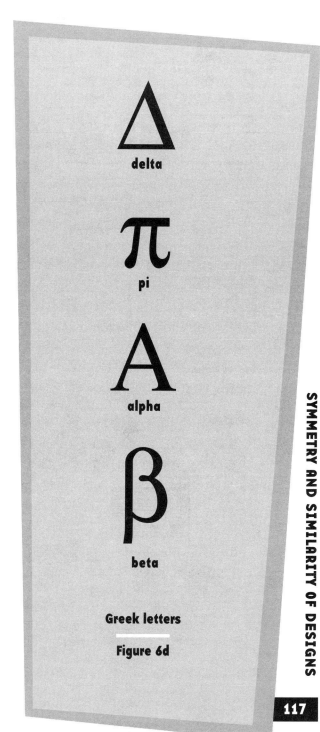

delta

pi

alpha

beta

**Greek letters**

**Figure 6d**

Figure 7a

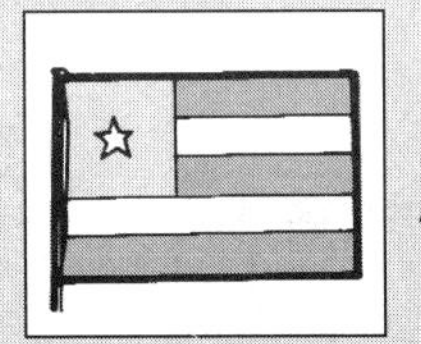

**Flag of Togo**

Figure 7b

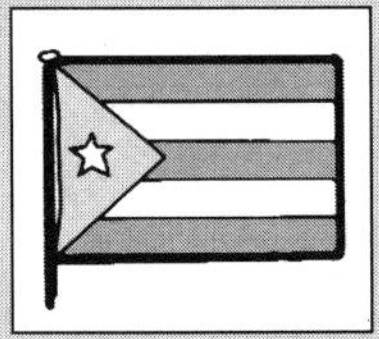

**Flag of Cuba or Puerto Rico**

Figure 7c

**Flag of Pakistan**

Figure 7d

**Flag of United States**

Figure 7e

# Flags with Stars from Many Countries

Find pictures of the flags of all the countries in the world. An almanac should have them. Look at the picture of the flag in **Figure 7a**. Try to match the picture with the flags in the almanac. You should find two flags that match: Somalia's and Vietnam's. The flag of Somalia has a white star on a blue background, while the Vietnamese flag has a yellow star on a red background. What did you look for when you tried to match flags to the picture? The five-pointed star is the only feature on both flags. The colors of the two flags are different, but colors don't show on a black and white picture.

You will find that many countries feature the five-pointed star on their flags. Some show one star against a background of stripes. An example is Suriname, a country in the northern part of South America. The Togo flag has one star in the corner. The red, white, and blue Cuban flag has a star in a triangular background, as does that of Puerto Rico. In fact, their flags are identical except that the red and blue are interchanged. It may be hard to find a picture of the flag of Puerto Rico because it is a commonwealth of the United States, not an independent country. The flag of Pakistan has a star and a crescent moon. **Figure 7b, 7c, 7d**

Some flags have more than one five-pointed star; Syria and Panama are examples. But no flag has as many stars as that of the United States! **Figure 7e**

You can design your own flag with the five-pointed star as a design. First practice drawing the star.

## MATERIALS
- Paper
- Pencil
- Eraser
- Compass
- Ruler
- Colored markers or crayons

## DRAWING A FIVE-POINTED STAR

**1.** Draw a circle with a radius of 2 inches (5 cm). Put a mark at the top of the circle. **Figure 8a**

**2.** Place the zero point of your ruler on that mark. Put a mark on the circle at the 2⅜-inch (5.8-cm) point on your ruler.

**3.** Continue to put marks on the circle that are 2⅜ inches (5.8 cm) apart. You should have five marks with equal distances between them. Label them in order: *A*, *B*, *C*, *D*, and *E*. **Figure 8b**

**4.** Connect the points in this order: A to C, C to E, E to B, B to D, D to A. Do this without lifting your pencil from the paper. **Figure 8c**

**5.** Now you have a five-pointed star. Color the star as you like, and design a flag around it.

## THINGS TO THINK ABOUT AND DO

**1.** Look at the pictures of the flags of all the countries. Find the flags that have a five-pointed star and a crescent moon, like the flag of Pakistan. Locate these countries on a map.

What is the meaning of the crescent moon? What part of their culture do most of these countries have in common?

**2.** Many African countries display the colors red, gold, and green in their flags. The flag of Ghana is a good example. These colors are symbolic for Africa. Red is for the blood shed in captivity, gold is for the wealth of Africa, and green stands for the vegetation of the land. Look at the flags of other African countries and note whether they use these colors.

**3.** Make a list of the flags that display more than one five-pointed star. Where are these countries located?

**4.** Some countries have flags with stars having more than five points. One example is the flag of Israel, with its six-pointed star. What is the significance of this star? **Figure 8d**

**5.** Examine the five-pointed star for symmetry. How many lines of symmetry does it have? In how many different positions does it look the same as you turn the paper?

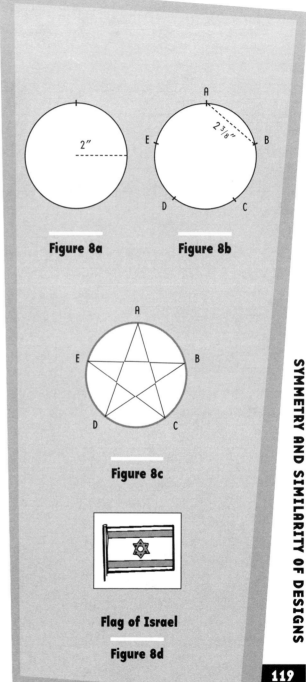

Figure 8a    Figure 8b

Figure 8c

Flag of Israel

Figure 8d

# Multiplying Five-Pointed Stars

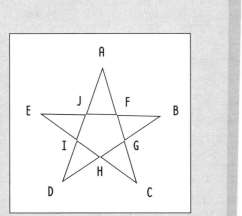

**Figure 9a**

**W**hen you drew the five-pointed star in the previous activity, were you able to do it without lifting your pencil from the paper? The figure you drew is called a pentagram. It is a very ancient sign. The people of ancient Babylon considered it a magic charm. To the Celtic priests of Ireland it was the witch's foot. Some believed this sign was a protection from demons and a symbol of safety. No wonder so many nations put it on their flags!

Now you will learn to make a lot of connected five-pointed stars without lifting your pencil from the paper.

## MATERIALS
- Plain paper
- Pencil
- Eraser
- Compass
- Ruler
- Colored pen or pencil

**1.** With a plain lead pencil, draw the five-pointed star with points at A, B, C, D, and E, according to the directions in the previous activity (page 119). Erase the circle.

**2.** Mark the points *F*, *G*, *H*, *I*, and *J*, as in **Figure 9a**.

**3.** Use a colored pencil to draw a small star in the branch with its point at A. Starting at point F, connect F to A, then A to J.

**4.** From J draw a line to point K, then from K to L, and back to F. All these lines should have the same length as the lines you drew in Step #3.

**Figure 9b**

**5.** With the colored pencil, connect F to G. Then, starting at G, draw a small star in the branch of the large star that has its point at B.

**6.** Continue by drawing a small star in each branch of the large star, until you return to the starting point F.

You have traced the entire large star while drawing the five small stars. You can carry out the whole process in one continuous line, without taking your pencil off the paper!

**Figure 9c**

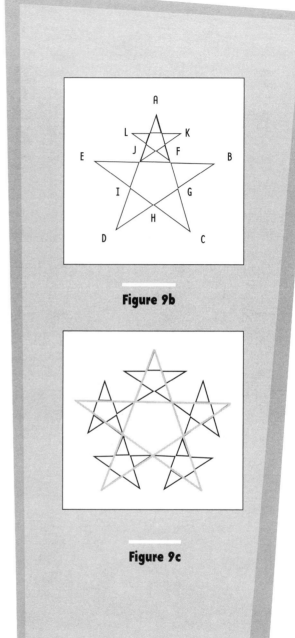

**Figure 9b**

**Figure 9c**

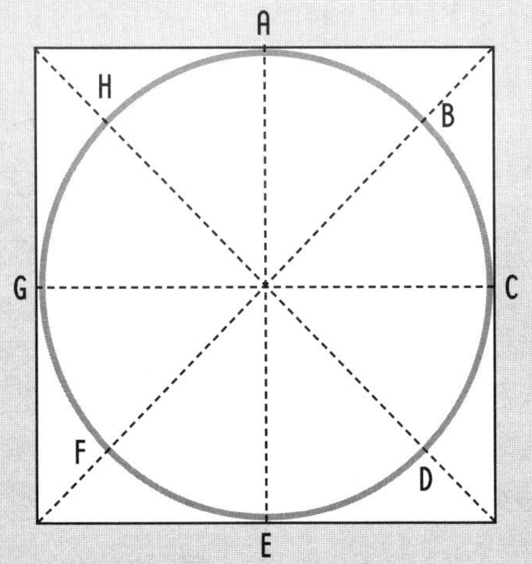

**Figure 10a**

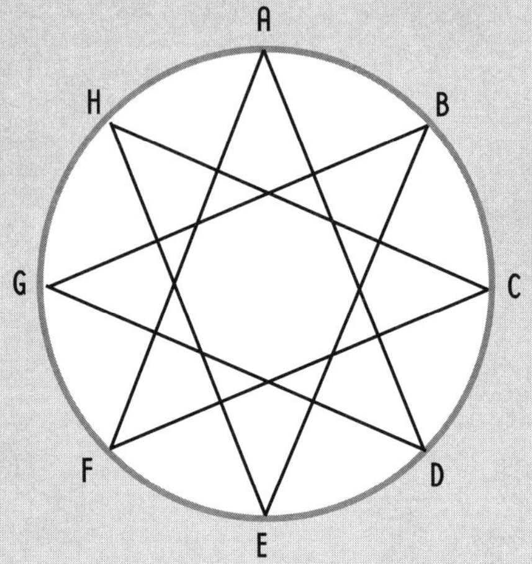

**Figure 10b**

# Drawing Stars with One Stroke

**N**ow that you have learned to draw a five-pointed star without lifting your pencil from the paper, you are ready to draw an eight-pointed star with one stroke of the pencil. Eight-pointed stars are very common in rugs, baskets, quilts, mats, and other handmade objects. Factory-made items often use the eight-pointed star as decoration. Later in this chapter you will learn how quilt makers use the eight-pointed star as a design element.

## MATERIALS
- Paper
- Pencil
- Ruler
- Compass
- Colored crayons or markers

## MAKING AN EIGHT-POINTED STAR
With this method you can construct the star without lifting your pencil from the paper.

**1.** Draw a large square. Lightly draw the two diagonals. Then draw light vertical and horizontal lines through the center.

**2.** Place the compass point in the center and draw a circle inside the square, touching the square at four points.

**3.** Label the points on the circle in order, starting with A and ending with H. **Figure 10a**

**4.** Use your ruler to draw lines connecting the points, as follows: A to D to G to B to E to H to C to F to A. In other words, skip two points as you draw the lines. The rule is to follow each line as far as it can go, from one point on the circle to another. You have completed the star in one stroke of your pencil. You may want to erase the unnecessary lines. **Figure 10b**

**5.** Color the star as you please.

## THINGS TO THINK ABOUT AND DO

**1.** Draw a seven-pointed star without lifting your pencil from the paper. Draw a circle and make seven equally spaced marks on it. Estimate the distances between the points, or use a protractor to measure 51 degrees of arc. Label the points in order from A to G. Then connect the marks, skipping two points each time. Always draw straight lines from one point on the circle to another. **Figure 11a**

**2.** Try to draw a six-pointed star, like the star on the flag of Israel, without lifting your pencil from the paper. Remember that you must draw straight lines from one point on a circle to another. It cannot be done in one stroke. Why not? **Figure 11b**

**3.** Examine each type of star for line (mirror) symmetry and for turn (rotational) symmetry.

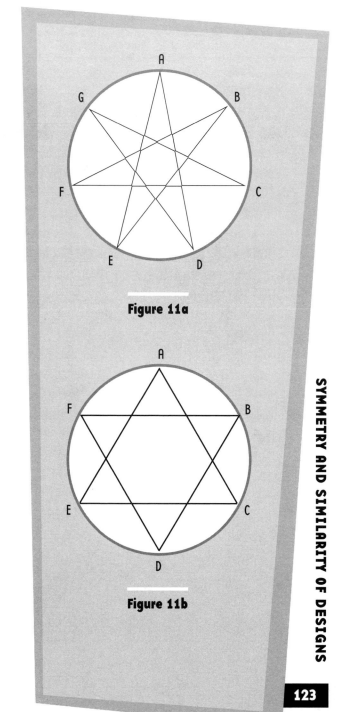

**Figure 11a**

**Figure 11b**

# Navajo Weaving from Native America

**Navajo rug**

---

**Figure 12a**

Source: From the collection of
Sophie and David Smith

The Navajo call themselves *Dine* (dee-NAY), a word that means "the people" in their language. For three centuries, Navajo women have been weaving beautiful blankets and rugs. These weavings, often called the "first American tapestries," have a well-deserved place in museums. The Navajo learned the technique of weaving from their neighbors, the Pueblo.

At first the women wove blankets to cover their families as they slept, as well as to hang on the walls to protect against cold weather. Later they began to weave rugs for sale to the public. Some rugs have simple geometric designs. Others are complicated (and expensive). It may take a woman several months to weave a small rug.

Navajo weavers don't work from written patterns or instructions. They memorize the designs and count carefully. Different communities within Navajo reservations have developed their own styles. Contests are held every year to reward the weavers of the most beautiful rugs in each style.

In the past, the wool was dyed in colors made from roots, berries, bark, fruit, and flowers. The most common colors were gray, black, tan, yellow, red, and brown, as well as white. Today the weavers may use factory-made synthetic dyes and more colors. **Figure 12a**

What do you notice about the rug in **Figure 12a**? It has several diamond-shaped designs of different sizes. These shapes are similar to one another. It also has several designs composed of similar triangles. The colors of these shapes are gray, black, and yellow, and they are set against a white background. **Figure 12b**

The rug in **Figure 12b** has a center design in black on white and four black geometric figures at the ends, on a tan background. There is also a repeated pattern to form a border in light brown on white. You may also see some small yellow and tan geometric figures around the center design.

## LOOK CAREFULLY—WHAT DO YOU SEE?

**1.** What is the shape of each rug?

**2.** Look at the rug in **Figure 12a**. Which designs appear more than once? Are they exactly the same? Handcrafted weavings often have slight flaws or differences in the designs that you don't see in factory-made rugs and other textiles. Do you think the weaver intended to make them exactly the same?

**3.** Now look at **Figure 12b** to see which designs are repeated, and how they are repeated.

**4.** Look for the similar shapes in each rug.

**5.** Examine each rug for line (mirror) symmetry and for turn (rotational) symmetry.

**6.** Analyze the design elements in each rug for symmetry.

## MAKE YOUR OWN NAVAJO RUG

## MATERIALS

- Plain paper or construction paper
- Colored construction paper in Navajo colors (optional)
- Pencil
- Ruler
- Colored crayons or markers in Navajo colors
- Scissors (optional)
- Glue stick or paste (optional)

**Navajo rug**

**Figure 12b**

Source: From the collection of Syrda Schnipper

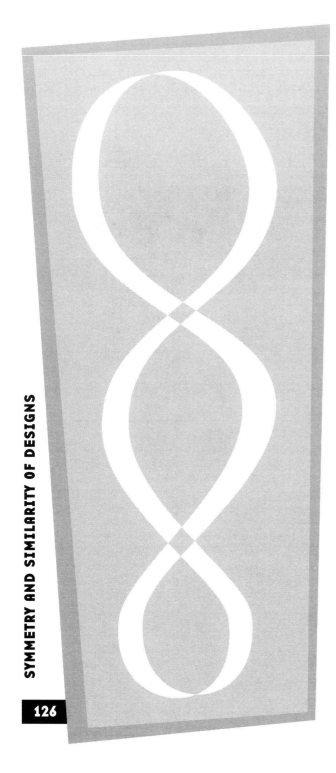

You can make your own rug of paper. One way is to draw the pattern on a rectangular sheet of paper and color it. Another way is to cut out several geometric designs from colored paper and glue them to a rectangular sheet. Decide which method you prefer. The materials you use will depend on the method. You can combine both methods—cut out and glue the larger design elements and draw a border with crayons or markers.

## THINGS TO THINK ABOUT AND DO

**1.** Locate the Navajo reservations on a map. They cover more than 24,000 square miles in northeastern Arizona, northwestern New Mexico, and southeastern Utah. The Navajo are the largest group of Native Americans in the United States. Many Navajo (Dine) speak their own language, as well as English.

**2.** Find photographs of Navajo rugs and other art objects.

**3.** Read the book *The Goat in the Rug*, by Charles Blood and Martin Link. Geraldine, a goat, tells about weaving a Navajo rug (see Bibliography page 156).

**4.** Look for *Navajo Rugs and Blankets: A Coloring Book*, by Chuck and Andrea Mobley (see Bibliography page 157) and other books about Navajo culture and history. Their relatives, the Dene (deh-NAY), live in Alaska. You may want to learn about their lives.

# Star-Patterned Patchwork Quilts from the United States

In colonial times and in the early days of the republic, women arranged quilting bees, social gatherings for the purpose of making quilts. They gathered together and planned their work. Each woman made several squares called quilt blocks. Then the women sewed them together to make a beautiful bed cover. Often they followed standard designs, but sometimes they made up their own. The eight-pointed star or starflower was a favorite.

Often the quilting bee was the only recreation that a woman had. The quilt might be a present for a newly married couple or a going-away gift for a family moving west. Quilts from many Native American communities have been exhibited at the National Museum of the American Indian. Quilts were associated with the Underground Railroad, the system of safe houses for slaves escaping to the North. A favorite pattern for these quilts was the Variable Star, more often called the Ohio Star. Elizabeth Keckley bought freedom from slavery for herself and her son with her beautiful quilt. Later she became the seamstress to the wife of President Lincoln. Today quilting is becoming more and more popular among many groups in the United States.

There are various ways to make an eight-pointed star or starflower quilt block. You might want to make several types of stars out of paper. Here are two ways. In the next activity you will learn another way.

## MATERIALS
- Several sheets of construction paper of different colors
- Pencil
- Ruler
- Markers or crayons (optional)
- Scissors

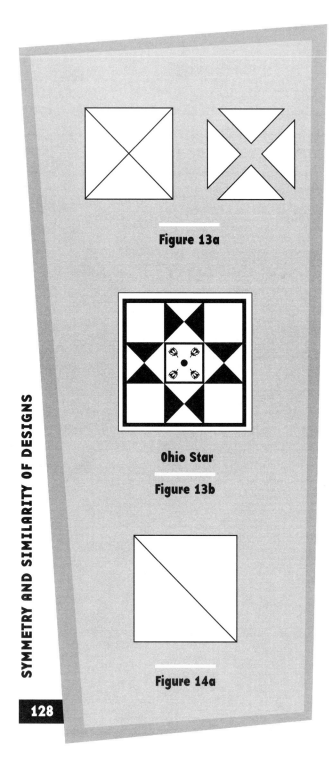

Figure 13a

Ohio Star

Figure 13b

Figure 14a

## MAKING A STAR QUILT BLOCK
## Method I: The Ohio Star
## (also called Variable Star)

This is the simplest design.

**1.** Use the pencil and ruler to draw two-inch (5 cm) squares on each of three sheets of paper of different colors.

**2.** Cut out five squares of color A, three squares of color B, and one square of color C.

**3.** Cut two squares of color B and one square of color C into quarters by cutting along the diagonals to make triangles. **Figure 13a**

**4.** Arrange the shapes as in **Figure 13b.**

**5.** Glue the shapes to a sheet of paper. You may want to add decorations and a border with your crayons or markers.

## Method II

This quilt block is copied from the work of an African American woman. She wrote her message in the center of the square.

**1.** Cut out eight 2-inch (5-cm) squares of one color and four of another color.

**2.** Cut four squares of each color in half along the diagonal. **Figure 14a**

**3.** Cut out a 4-inch (10-cm) square of white or light paper. Write a message or poem on the paper, and sign your name and date.

**4.** Arrange the squares as in **Figure 14b** and glue them to another sheet of paper.

**5.** You may prefer to use triangles in different combinations of colors to make a starflower, as in **Figure 14c**.

## THINGS TO THINK ABOUT AND DO

**1.** Analyze the two star designs for line symmetry and turn symmetry. Look at the shapes and the colors. Consider both the star design alone and the whole quilt block.

**2.** Read the book *Shota and the Star Quilt*, by Margaret Bateson-Hill (see Bibliography). Shota, a Lakota girl and her friend solve their housing problem when they make a star quilt. The opening lines are:

"Find the star that's a gift from the skies.

In its patchwork of light true happiness lies."

**3.** Learn about the various types of quilts designed by Native American, African American, and European American women. Are they similar or different?

**4.** Read *Eight Hands Round* by Ann W. Paul (see Bibliography) to learn about quilts in the Underground Railroad.

**5.** Read the book *Tar Beach*, by the African American artist Faith Ringgold (see Bibliography). The illustration she uses is her painted, pieced, and printed quilt that tells a story of her childhood in New York City. (Additional books about patchwork are listed in the Bibliography.)

**6.** Invent your own quilt block designs. If you have pattern blocks or attribute blocks, you can use them to make a variety of designs.

**7.** Work with your friends to make a wall hanging of several quilt blocks attached to a large sheet of paper or cloth.

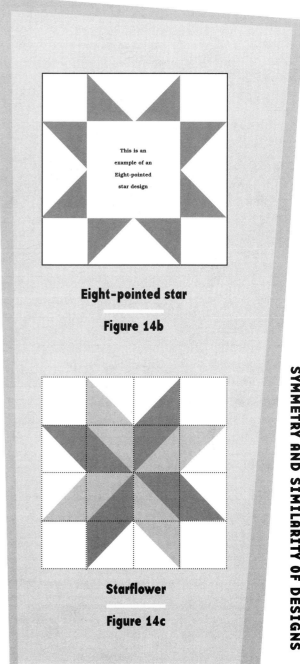

This is an example of an Eight-pointed star design

**Eight-pointed star**

**Figure 14b**

**Starflower**

**Figure 14c**

# More Patchwork Quilt Designs

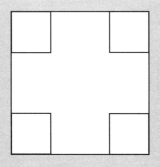

**Figure 15a**

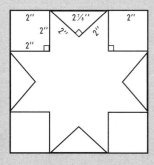

**Figure 15b**

**H**ere is another way to make a starflower design. With this method, you will form the part of the quilt block that is not the starflower. The leftover part of the block will be the starflower!

## MATERIALS

- Sheet of white or light-colored construction paper
- Pencil
- Ruler
- Small piece of heavy paper or cardboard
- Scissors
- Colored markers or crayons

**1.** On the sheet of paper use your pencil to draw a square measuring 6⅞ inches (17 cm) on a side.

**2.** Cut out a 2-inch (5-cm) square from heavy paper or cardboard.

**3.** Use the small square to trace a square at each corner of the large square. **Figure 15a**

**4.** Place the small square diagonally on the space between the squares you drew and trace the triangle, as in **Figure 15b**. Do this on each side of the large square. **Figure 15b**

**5.** You now have the outline of the starflower. Draw lines to separate the eight petals, as in **Figure 15c**. You may also want to draw the small star inside the large one.

**6.** Color the design and the background. You might want to add decorations and a border to the quilt block.

### THINGS TO THINK ABOUT AND DO

**1.** Analyze the star design for symmetry. You should be able to find eight lines of symmetry. You should also see that the design looks the same in eight different positions as you rotate it.

**2.** Analyze **Figure 15c** for similarity.

**3.** The star design is very popular with quilt makers. It has had many different meanings. Find other examples of quilts using the star design.

**4. Figure 16** is a simple version of the quilt block design called Monkey Wrench. Why do you think it has that name? It is made on a 3 × 3 quilt block. You will need four triangles and four rectangles of each color, and an additional square of one of the colors. Figure out how to make this quilt block.

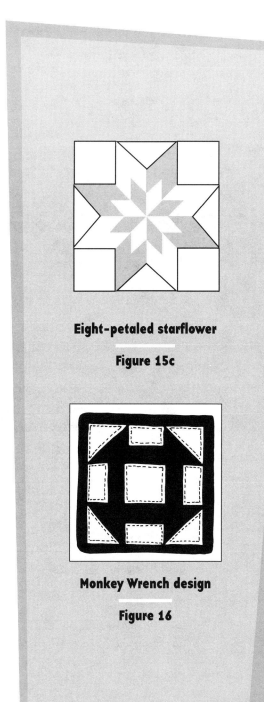

**Eight-petaled starflower**

**Figure 15c**

**Monkey Wrench design**

**Figure 16**

**Kuba raffia velour**

**Figure 1a**

Source: From Geoffrey Williams,
*African Designs*

**Patterns on a Benin bronze lamp**

**Figure 1b**

Source: Based on drawing by D. W. Crowe,
in Claudia Zaslavsky, *Africa Counts*

# Repeated Patterns

Repeated patterns are all around you. Look at a brick wall or a tiled floor. The paving blocks in the sidewalk are another example. Maybe you try to step on the lines or skip over the lines as you walk.

In this chapter most of the examples will be about repeated patterns as decorations. The Kuba people of the Democratic Republic of Congo, in Central Africa, have long been famous for their beautiful patterned cloth and carved wooden objects. **Figure 1a** shows the pattern on a piece of woven raffia cloth, often called "Kuba velour" because it is soft and thick. Note how the same designs are repeated over and over again.

Benin City, in Nigeria, West Africa, produced fine bronze objects. All the border patterns that you see in **Figure 1b** are from a bronze lamp with eight arms. Here you see each design repeated along a line.

In this chapter you will see many examples of repeated patterns in borders and over whole surfaces. These examples are from different parts of the world.

Hand-painted cloth from Nigeria displays a variety of designs and patterns, while a single design is embroidered over and over again in the Japanese craft called *sashiko*. Then there's the fantastic work of Islamic artists in the architecture of Spain and in the tiny hand-painted pictures in books of ancient Persia, now called Iran.

The chapter ends with fractals in Native American basket weaving. What are fractals? You will find out!

# Embroidery from Hungary

When I was in Hungary a few years ago, I bought a beautiful scarf to cover my chest of drawers. Most of the scarf is bright red, with stripes of black, red, and white running across it. At each end is a border in red, white, and black, as in **Figure 2a**. The weaver used a sewing needle threaded with strands of red or black wool to embroider the repeated pattern on the white background. She was very careful to repeat the design over and over again. Clusters of red wool fringe hang from the border. Farm women wove and embroidered beautiful patterned cloth after their farmwork and housework were done.

Look carefully at each of the repeated patterns. Then analyze each design for line (or mirror) symmetry and for turn (or rotational) symmetry. (See page 106 to read more about symmetry.) Make sure you analyze each of these designs or repeated patterns:

**1.** Eight-pointed starflower

**2.** V-shaped design, right side up and upside down

**3.** Row of zigzags

**4.** Tiny crosses or plus signs

**5.** Row of flowers between the two rows of V-shaped figures

**6.** Any other patterns you can find

How is each type of repeated pattern related to some of the others?

You can design a border pattern in the style of the Hungarian embroidered border. Before you start to draw, think about the designs you want to repeat to make the border.

## MATERIALS
- Several sheets of plain white paper or graph paper
- Pencil
- Ruler

**Hungarian border patterns**

**Figure 2a**

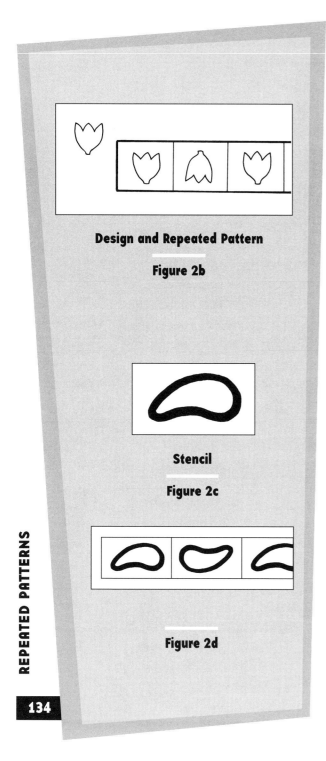

**Design and Repeated Pattern**

**Figure 2b**

**Stencil**

**Figure 2c**

**Figure 2d**

- Crayons or colored markers
- Cardboard or Styrofoam
- Scissors

## MAKE YOUR OWN REPEATED PATTERN

**1.** On a sheet of paper, make a rough sketch of the border you have in mind. Will you have just one row of a repeated design, or more than one, like the Hungarian border?

**2.** On your graph paper or plain paper, use the pencil to draw two parallel lines to make a track. You will make your repeated pattern between the two lines. Divide the space between the two lines into rectangles of the same size. Draw the lines lightly.

**3.** Decide on the method you will use to repeat your design. Here are two possible methods.

*Tracing method.* Cut a design out of cardboard or Styrofoam. Trace your design in pencil in the center of the first rectangle. Use your ruler to measure the distances, or count spaces on graph paper. When you do the next rectangle, you may want to turn your design upside down, or flip it over sideways, or rotate it a half turn. **Figure 2b**

*Stencil method.* Cut a rectangle of cardboard or Styrofoam to match the rectangles in your track. Cut a design in the rectangle to use as a pattern. **Figure 2c**

With your pencil, trace the design in the first rectangle of your track. You may want to turn the stencil upside down or flip it over in the second rectangle. **Figure 2d**

**4.** Color your pattern. You might add some decorations.

**5.** Draw another row of repeated patterns, using a different design.

## THINGS TO THINK ABOUT AND DO

**1.** Find Hungary on a map of Europe.

**2.** Look for pictures of woven cloth with borders of repeated patterns. Find examples of clothing, place mats, or other items with border patterns. How are the designs repeated?

**3.** Do you know how to embroider? Try to embroider a border pattern on a piece of cloth. First plan how you will do it.

# Tessellations–Repeating the Design

ook at a brick wall. What shapes do you see? The side of the brick is in the shape of a rectangle, and this rectangular shape is repeated over and over again. **Figure 3a**

My bathroom floor is more interesting. It is covered with small square tiles, mostly gray, but with a white one at regular intervals. Look for floors with patterns of tiles. **Figure 3b**

Repeated patterns that cover whole surfaces are called *tessellations.* You can discover which geometric shapes can tessellate—that is, those that can cover a whole surface. You know that rectangles tessellate, as shown by the brick wall.

Squares, which are special rectangles, also tessellate. A sheet of graph paper is a good example. How about triangles and other shapes? You can carry out an experiment to find out.

## EXPERIMENT: SHAPES THAT TESSELLATE

## MATERIALS
- Several sheets of plain paper
- Cardboard or Styrofoam
- Pencil
- Ruler
- Crayons or colored markers
- Scissors

**Brick wall**

**Figure 3a**

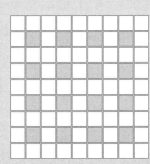

**Bathroom floor**

**Figure 3b**

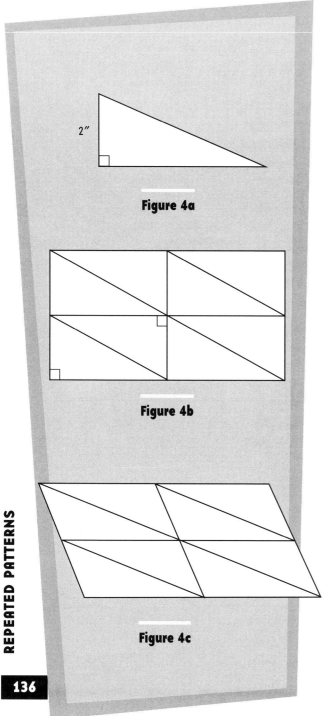

Figure 4a

Figure 4b

Figure 4c

**1.** Draw a right-angled triangle on cardboard (use the corner of the sheet of cardboard). The short leg should be about 2 inches (5 cm) long. Cut it out. **Figure 4a**

Trace the triangle on paper several times so that there are no spaces in between and sides of the same length are lined up. **Figure 4b**

You can see that a right triangle does tessellate. Color your tessellation.

**2.** On cardboard or Styrofoam, draw an obtuse triangle, one in which one angle is greater than 90 degrees. Cut it out. Trace the triangle on paper several times so that there are no spaces in between. This triangle also tessellates. Color your tessellation in contrasting colors. **Figure 4c**

**3.** How about four-sided shapes? You know that a rectangle tessellates. How about a parallelogram? Look at the tessellation in **Figure 4c**. Two adjoining triangles form a parallelogram. A rectangle is a special kind of parallelogram. You can color **Figure 4c** to bring out the shape of the parallelograms.

**4.** Experiment with other shapes. Does every four-sided figure tessellate? How about five-sided and six-sided shapes? Does a circle tessellate? Find out.

## THINGS TO THINK ABOUT AND DO

**1.** Do you have a set of pattern blocks? If you have, make tessellations by repeating each shape in turn. You should find that each shape tessellates. Then try to combine two different shapes; for example, can you make a tessellation with a combination of squares and triangles? How must the size of the square relate to the sides of the triangle?

**2.** Read the book *A Cloak for the Dreamer*, by Aileen Friedman (listed in the Bibliography under "Books for Kids"). The story is about a tailor and his three sons. The two older sons want to be tailors, and they design patchwork coats to show their skill. The oldest, Ivan, makes his cloak of rectangles, like brickwork. The second son, Alex, uses triangles for one cloak and squares for another. But Misha, the youngest, dreams of going out into the world. He makes his cloak of circles. Of course, it cannot be worn because it is full of holes. The father and the two older sons solve the problem. They cut each circle into a hexagon (six-sided shape), sew them together, and give the finished cloak to the youngest to keep him warm on his travels. Why does the hexagon shape solve the problem?

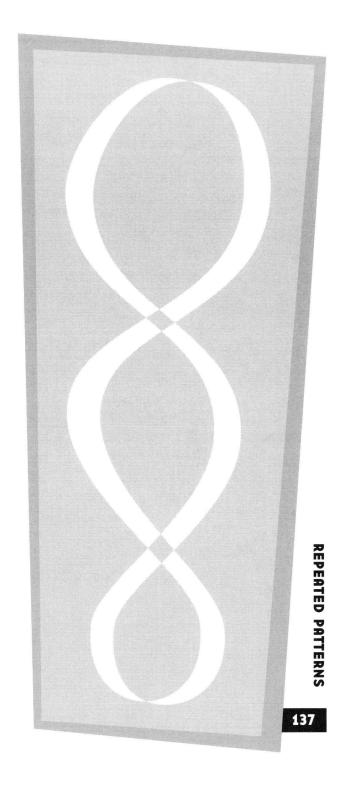

# Adire Cloth from Nigeria

**Starch-dyed adire cloth**

**Figure 5a**

**W**hen I visited Nigeria, I watched a Yoruba woman prepare *adire* (ah-DEE-ra) cloth. The *Yoruba* (YOR-ah-ba) people live in the southwestern part of Nigeria, in West Africa. They have their own language and culture, different from other ethnic groups in Nigeria. Yoruba clothing, for both women and men, can be very elegant. Adire cloth is one part of the costume.

The word *adire* means "to tie and dye." Some adire is made by that method. The *aladire*, the person who makes adire cloth, ties the designs into plain white cloth and sends it to a dyer to be dyed, usually blue. The tied parts remain white. After the cloth has been tied and dyed several times, she cuts the threads and sells the cloth in the market.

The woman I watched was using a different method. She was designing a pattern for *adire eleko*, starch-dye cloth. The photograph (**Figure 5a**) shows a corner of a large piece of

this cloth. She divides a length of white cloth into rectangles. Each rectangle has a different design. The cloth in the photograph has many rectangles. The pattern is called "Ibadan is beautiful." Ibadan is the largest city in the Yoruba region of Nigeria.

To make the design, the aladire mixes flour and water to make a thick starchy paste. Then she dips her feather or stick into the paste and paints the design on the cloth. She doesn't use a ruler or refer to a pattern. It is all in her memory and her imagination. Some designs date back many years, while others tell of events that just happened or describe some part of the woman's life. When the cloth is dyed, usually dark blue, the painted parts remain white or pale blue. We say that the painted parts resist the dye. The dye comes from the indigo plant. **Figure 5a**

Look at the large rectangle in the lower left part of the photo. It is made up of a lot of triangles. Do you see small squares formed from two triangles, one dark and the other light? Can you find pinwheels within larger squares?

Look along the diagonals. Do you see the medium-size squares formed from four triangles, two light and two dark? You can find several different repeated patterns in that large rectangle.

## MATERIALS

- Pencil
- Ruler
- Plain white paper
- Dark blue marker or crayon

## MAKE AN ADIRE PATTERN

**1.** Use your pencil and ruler to draw a four-inch (10-cm) square, and divide it into 16 one-inch (2.5-cm) squares. **Figure 6a**

**2.** Draw diagonals, so that each square is divided into two triangles. **Figure 6b**

**3.** Color half the triangles blue and decorate the white triangles. **Figure 6c**

Do you see the pinwheels? Do you see small squares, medium squares, and large squares? **Figure 6d**

Now you are an aladire, a maker of adire cloth.

## THINGS TO THINK ABOUT AND DO

**1.** Find photographs of different types of cloth from Africa. Notice the patterns and symmetry.

**2.** Locate Nigeria on a map of Africa. Find Ibadan, in the southwest region. The nearby town of Abeokuta is the center of adire making.

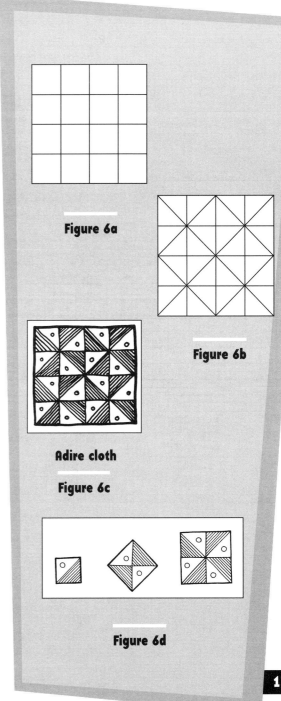

**Figure 6a**

**Figure 6b**

**Adire cloth**

**Figure 6c**

**Figure 6d**

# Sashiko Embroidery from Japan – Part I

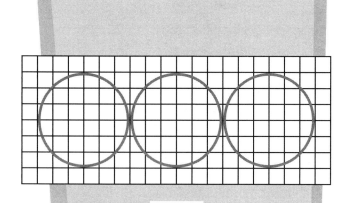

**Figure 7a**

**S**ashiko (SAH-shee-koh) is the name of a type of embroidery that Japanese mothers teach their daughters. When you see a Japanese name that ends in -ko, you know that it probably relates to girls and women. Sashiko patterns are based on geometric figures. The designs are inspired by nature and the environment—ocean waves, leaves of plants, tortoise shells—and are repeated over and over again. They are outlined with white thread in running stitches on blue cloth. In the old days, the dye came from the indigo plant. Today, factory-dyed cloth is common. Sashiko stitching in quilts and clothing makes the cloth stronger and helps it to wear longer.

You can practice making the patterns on paper. Once you have learned how to make them, you may want to transfer them to cloth and do the embroidery.

A popular pattern is Seven Treasures, based on interlocking circles. The same pattern is known as the Double Wedding Ring pattern among American quilters. This is an easy pattern to draw, and we will start with it.

## MATERIALS
- Graph paper
- Pencil
- Compass or jar lid
- Blue markers or crayons

## DRAWING SASHIKO REPEATED PATTERNS—SEVEN TREASURES

**1.** On graph paper, draw a circle about 2 inches (5 cm) in diameter. The size of the circle is not important. What is important is that the diameter is the length of an even number of spaces on the graph paper.

**2.** Using the same diameter, draw two more circles in a row touching one another. We say the circles are tangent to one another. **Figure 7a**

**3.** With the same diameter, draw full circles, half circles, and quarter circles that go through the tangent points of the first set of circles. Continue to draw circles, until your drawing looks like **Figure 7b**.

**4.** Color your pattern. Do you see four-petaled flowers?

I saw this repeating pattern on a 300-year-old red and gold robe in a museum. Within each curved space was a small gold flower with four petals, as in **Figure 7c**.

## THINGS TO THINK ABOUT AND DO

Find illustrations of Japanese robes and other embroidered clothing. What patterns do you see?

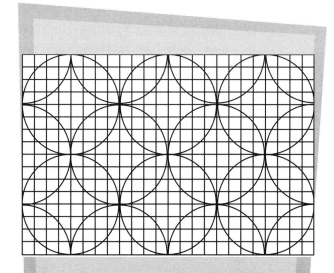

**Seven Treasures pattern**

**Figure 7b**

**Figure 7c**

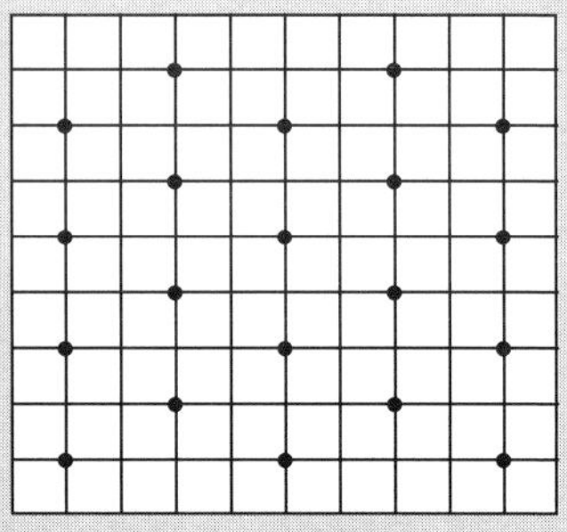

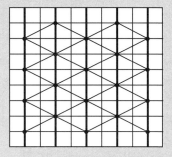

**Figure 8a**

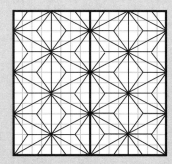

**Figure 8b**

**Hemp Leaf pattern**

**Figure 8c**

# Sashiko Embroidery from Japan – Part II

There are many different patterns of sashiko. The most common is the Hemp Leaf, probably because it strengthens the cloth so well. It is often used to make quilts.

## MATERIALS
- Graph paper
- Pencil
- Ruler
- Blue crayons or markers

## DRAWING THE HEMP LEAF PATTERN

**1.** Along the left side of the graph paper, make a column of dots, equally spaced. Let's say they are four spaces apart. You may choose any even number of spaces, depending upon the type of graph paper you use.

**2.** Move four spaces (or whatever number you use) to the right and make another column of dots, starting two spaces (half of four) above the first set of dots. Continue for several more columns. **Figure 8a**

**3.** Connect the dots with vertical straight lines and diagonal straight lines. **Figure 8b**

**4.** Fill in the remaining lines, as in **Figure 8c**. Draw the horizontal lines first, then connect them to make rhombus shapes.

**5.** Color your pattern. Do you see flowers with six petals?

## THINGS TO THINK ABOUT AND DO

The Chinese have been making tie-dyed indigo cloth for a long time. The earliest example came from a tomb dated to the year 683. In Japan this type of cloth is called *shibori*. Find Japan and China on the map. Do you think there is a connection between the Chinese and the Japanese customs of tie-dyed indigo cloth?

# Islamic Art from Spain

The Islamic religion was founded in the seventh century in the Middle East. In the following centuries the Islamic religion and culture spread from Spain to India, through North Africa and Turkey. The Islamic culture included artists, scientists, and mathematicians of different religions. Many were Muslims—followers of Islam—others were Christian or Jewish, or followers of other religions. The Arabic language was the language of science at that time.

Some branches of Islam did not allow pictures of people or animals. Such pictures could be considered as worshiping idols, which was not permitted. Artists drew geometric patterns using only a compass and a straightedge (an unmarked ruler). With these instruments alone they designed beautiful mosaics, collections of colored tiles inlaid on a flat surface. The tiles covered the entire surface, with no gaps. The same design was repeated over and over again to form a tessellation. The walls of mosques and palaces are covered with such tessellations.

Several years ago I visited the Alhambra, a complex of buildings in the town of Granada, in southern Spain. Muslims from North Africa had ruled the region from the eighth century until they were expelled in 1492. The palaces of the Alhambra display some of the most beautiful Islamic art in the world.

The tiled wall in **Figure 9** is in the Hall of Repose, where the king and his court rested after their bath and musicians played soothing music in the gallery above. The design is based on "flying triangles," triangles that appear to be floating through the air. Their colors are light blue, deep blue, golden brown, and white. The white spaces between the tiles are actually white flying triangles.

**Flying Triangles mosaic from the Alhambra**

**Figure 9**

REPEATED PATTERNS

143

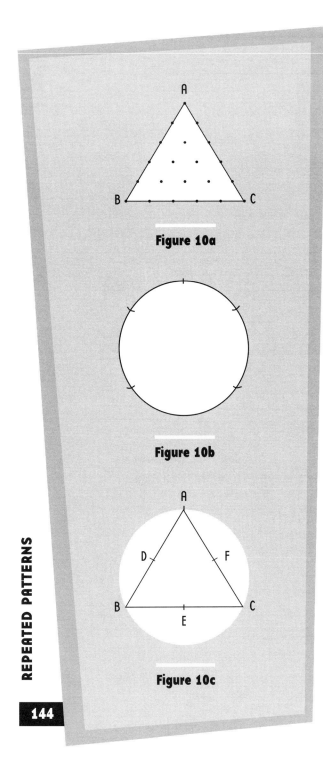

**Figure 10a**

**Figure 10b**

**Figure 10c**

You can draw a lovely mosaic of flying triangles.

## MATERIALS
- Cardboard or Styrofoam
- Plain white paper or triangular (isometric) graph paper
- White or light-colored construction paper
- Pencil
- Compass
- Ruler
- Scissors
- Glue (optional)
- Crayons or colored markers

## DRAWING FLYING TRIANGLES

First you will make a template, or pattern, of cardboard or Styrofoam. Then you will trace the template as many times as you like.

**1.** If you use triangular (isometric) graph paper, cut a square about four inches (10 cm) on the side and glue it to the cardboard. Draw an equilateral triangle about two inches (5 cm) on the side. An equilateral triangle has three equal sides and three equal angles, just like the small units of the graph paper. Label the vertices with the letters A, B, and C. **Figure 10a**

If you use plain paper, follow these directions:

**a.** On the cardboard or Styrofoam draw a circle with a diameter of about 2¼ inches (6 cm). Make a mark on the circle. Using the same radius, place the compass point on that mark and mark two points. Place the compass point on each of these points and mark two more points. **Figure 10b**

**b.** With the ruler, draw lines connecting three points on the circle to form an equilateral triangle. Label the vertices A, B, and C. Erase the circle.

**2.** Mark and label the midpoint of each side. **Figure 10c**

**3.** Place the compass point on the midpoint D of side AB. Draw an arc going through points B and E. Place the compass point on E and draw an arc going through points C and F. Then place the compass point on F and draw an arc through points A and D. **Figure 10d**

**4.** Use the same radius on the compass. Place the point outside the triangle so that an arc passes through points D and B. Draw a similar arc through points E and C, and another arc through F and A. **Figure 10e**

**5.** Cut out the flying triangle template. **Figure 10f**

**6.** Trace the template on the construction paper. Then turn the template upside down, place it next to the triangle on the paper, and trace it. Continue until you have many triangles to form a mosaic. **Figure 10g**

**7.** Color the alternate triangles. **Figure 10h**

## THINGS TO THINK ABOUT AND DO

**1.** On a map, find the lands that were under Islamic influence a thousand years ago.

**2.** Look for more examples of Islamic art, from the Alhambra and elsewhere. Besides geometric shapes, Islamic artists often used plant life and Arabic inscriptions from the Quran, the holy book of Islam.

**3.** The twentieth-century Dutch artist M. C. Escher visited the Alhambra, and the experience changed his life. He became a master of the most unusual kinds of tessellations, using birds, fish, insects, and other creatures as the design motif. Find examples of Escher's work and try to analyze them.

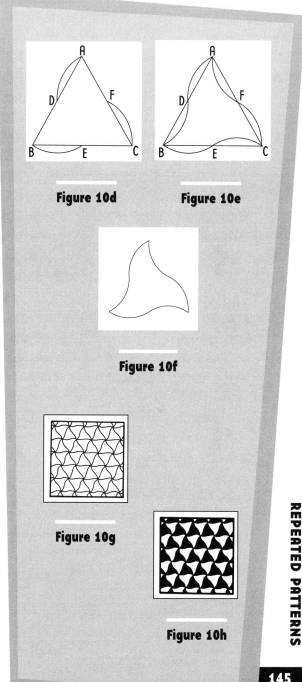

**Figure 10d**          **Figure 10e**

**Figure 10f**

**Figure 10g**

**Figure 10h**

# Islamic Art from Iran (formerly Persia)

**Adapted from the Shāh-nāmeh, the Book of Kings**

**Figure 11**

Source: *Multicultural Mathematics* by Claudia Zaslavsky, published by J. Weston Walch

The country of Persia, now called Iran, was famous for its beautiful hand-painted books telling the history of the kings and their people. **Figure 11** is a copy of the tiled wall in a painting in the *Shāh-nāmeh*, the Book of Kings. **Figure 11**

What geometric shapes do you see in the illustration? Find the stars. Each star is made up of a hexagon and six triangles. Diamond-shaped **figures** called rhombuses, or rhombi (plural of "rhombus"), surround each star. Notice how the clever artist used the same rhombi to form parts of the borders for more than one star. The same pattern is repeated to cover the whole surface and form a tessellation.

You can copy this beautiful tessellation. To do this, you will first make templates for the hexagon, the triangle, and the rhombus.

**MATERIALS**
- Plain white paper or construction paper
- Cardboard or Styrofoam
- Pencil
- Compass
- Ruler
- Scissors
- Crayons or colored markers

## DRAWING AN ISLAMIC TESSELLATION

**1.** Open the compass to a radius of about 1½ inches (4 cm). Draw a circle on the cardboard or Styrofoam.

**2.** Make a mark on the circle. With the same radius on the compass, place the compass point on that mark and make two marks on the circumference. Place the compass point on each of the marks you made, and make two more marks on the circumference. Then repeat to make another mark on the circumference. **Figure 12a**

**3.** Draw lines connecting the six points on the circle to make a regular hexagon—all the sides are equal and all the angles are congruent (equal). **Figure 12b**

**4.** Cut out the hexagon. Trace it on the cardboard and cut out this second hexagon.

**5.** Cut the second hexagon in half to form two trapezoids. **Figure 12c**

**6.** See the diagram of the trapezoid (**Figure 12d**). Measure the line from A to B on one trapezoid. Make a mark, E, so that BE equals AB. Draw a line connecting point E to point A. **Figure 12d**

**7.** Cut out equilateral triangle ABE. The remaining shape AECD is a rhombus.

**8.** Use the templates of the hexagon, triangle, and rhombus to copy the pattern from the Book of Kings (**Figure 11**) and color it. You may want to add decorations to some of the shapes.

## THINGS TO THINK ABOUT AND DO

**1.** Invent your own repeated pattern using any or all four of the templates.

**2.** Find photographs of Persian manuscripts. Note that these Islamic artists did draw pictures of human beings and animals, although some branches of Islam did not permit such pictures to be drawn.

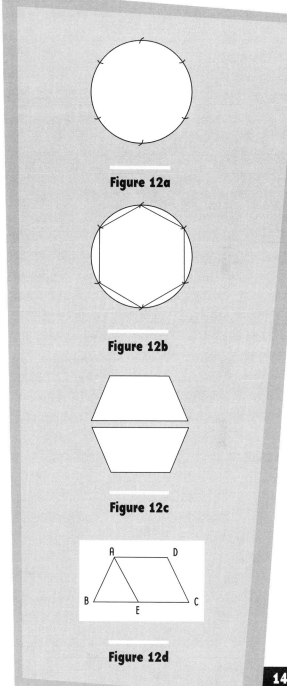

**Figure 12a**

**Figure 12b**

**Figure 12c**

**Figure 12d**

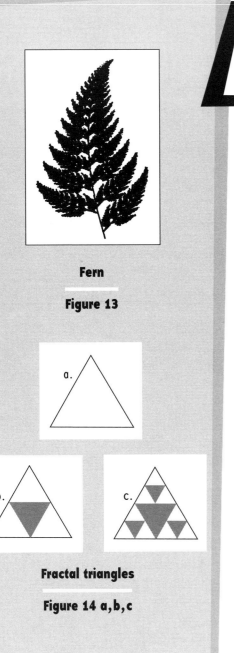

**Fern**

Figure 13

**Fractal triangles**

Figure 14 a,b,c

# Fractal Patterns from Native North America

**N**ature is strange and wonderful. Look at the picture of a fern. Each little branch of the fern is similar to the whole fern. **Figure 13**

Look at the large triangle. We can divide it into four similar smaller triangles. The middle triangle is dark. Then repeat the process with each of the three white triangles. This process can go on and on. We call this type of repetition a *fractal* pattern. The original design repeats itself on a smaller and smaller scale. **Figures 14a**, **14b**, **14c**

**Figure 15** is a picture of a basket made by the Native American Maidu people. The word *Maidu* means "the people" in their language. They lived in the Sacramento Valley in California. Their staple food was acorns, which they gathered in baskets in the autumn and stored for the coming winter. Once the acorns were ground up, they were eaten as cereal, soup, or bread.

Unfortunately for the Maidu, they contracted malaria from a hunting party in 1833, and many died. Then gold was discovered on their land in 1848. Hordes of men from the East rushed to California to make their fortunes. Native people like the Maidu were killed or driven off their land. Their children were forced into slavery. Native people did not profit from the gold.

Examine the Maidu basket. Do you see fractal patterns of triangles? Most of the triangles are equilateral—all three sides are equal. Some triangles are not equilateral. Remember that such baskets are handwoven. Perhaps the basket weaver intended to make them equilateral. What do you think?

## THINGS TO THINK ABOUT AND DO

**1.** Imagine that you live in a Maidu village just as the California gold rush is starting. What do you think you and your family would do? Read about the California gold rush. Most accounts do not even mention that Native Americans lived in the region.

**2.** Design a place mat or other object with a fractal pattern. First decide upon your design element.

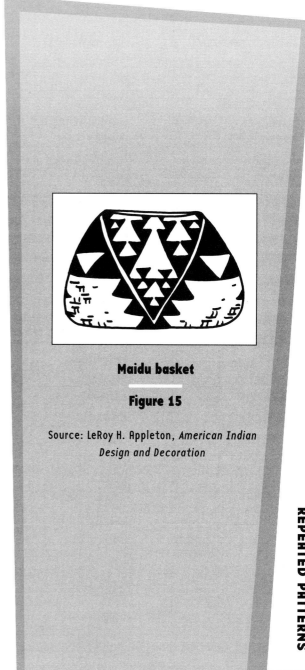

**Maidu basket**

**Figure 15**

Source: LeRoy H. Appleton, *American Indian Design and Decoration*

*More Math Games and Activities from Around the World* ©2003. Published by Chicago Review Press, Inc., 800-888-4741.

# Selected Answers

You probably are smart enough not to need many answers. Many of the activities are self-checking and you can figure out the reason if the outcome seems wrong. Finding your own mistakes gives you a feeling of success and is a lot more challenging than looking in the back of the book for the answer.

Here are some answers to help you check your work.

## CHAPTER 1
### Shape of the Board (page 26)
Triangle: 16; pentagon: 28; hexagon: 34

## CHAPTER 3
### The Calendar of the Maya (page 49)
1. a. 3,738 days
   b. 6,009 days
   c. 5,383 days
3. 18,132 days, or more than 49 years, including 12 leap years (13, if the first year is a leap year). Therefore 18,132 days = 49 years and 235 days.

### Wampum, Cocoa Beans, and Pieces of Eight (page 49)
1. a. 36 strings
   b. 316 strings
5. One quarter = 25 cents, or one quarter of a dollar; 12 bits

### Save Those Cans (page 58)
1. 260 cans
2. 975 hours, or 195 days if TV sets run 5 hours per day
3. About three billion gallons

### Saving the Lives of Children (page 60)
1. 2,000 ORT packets; 2,500 supplies of vitamin A; 16 sets of warm clothes; seeds for over 10,000 pounds of food

## CHAPTER 4
### Magic Squares from China and the Muslim World (page 70)
4. 4a

| 8 | 1 | 6 |
|---|---|---|
| 3 | 5 | 7 |
| 4 | 9 | 2 |

4b

| 4 | 9 | 2 |
|---|---|---|
| 3 | 5 | 7 |
| 8 | 1 | 6 |

## CHAPTER 5
### Save the Water (page 78)
1. 40 cups = 2½ gallons
2. 39 cups
3. 78 cups per day; 546 cups = 34⅛ gallons per week; 28,470 cups = 1,779 gallons per year

## CHAPTER 6
### Möbius Strip Surprises (page 96)
When you cut the strip through the middle, the result is a loop twice as long but half as wide as the original. When you cut one-third of the way from the edge, the outcome is two connected loops. One is twice the length of the original strip and the other is the same length as the original. Both are one-third the width of the original strip.

### Sand Drawings—Part I:
Animal Pictures, Things to Think About (page 98)
1. Two lines of symmetry; two turn positions
2. No line of symmetry; two positions in which the figure looks the same as it is turned

## CHAPTER 7
### Native American Beadwork—Part I (page 108)
3. 100 beads
5. 400 beads
6. Four

### Native American Beadwork—Part II (page 110)
3. 4¼ square cm; 128 beads

# Bibliography

## BOOKS AND ARTICLES FOR ADULTS

*Appleton, LeRoy. *American Indian Design and Decoration.* New York: Dover, 1971.

*Arai, Lucy. "A Sashiko Hanten (Short Jacket) to Stitch." *Piecework* Vol. 11 (September/October 1994): pp. 30–37.

*Ascher, Marcia. "Learning with Games of Strategy from Mongolia." *Teaching Children Mathematics* Vol. 8 (October 2001): pp. 96–99.

*———. *Mathematics Elsewhere.* Princeton, NJ: Princeton University Press, 2002.

Bazin, Maurice, Modesto Tamez & the Exploratorium Teacher Institute. *Mathematics and Science Across Cultures.* New York: The New Press, 2002.

*Béart, Charles. *Jeux et Jouets de l'Oest Africain.* Dakar, Senegal: IFAN, 1955.

*Bell, Robbie & Michael Cornelius. *Board Games Around the World.* New York: Cambridge University Press, 1988.

*Centner, Th. *L'enfant Africain et ses Jeux.* Elisabethville, Congo: CEPSI, 1963.

Closs, M. *Native American Mathematics.* Austin, TX: University of Texas Press, 1986.

*Gerdes, Paulus. "Exploring the Game of Julirde." *Teaching Children Mathematics* Vol. 7 (February 2001): pp. 321–327.

*———. *Geometry from Africa.* Washington, DC: Mathematical Association of America, 1999.

Grunfeld, Frederic, ed. *Games of the World.* New York: Ballantine, 1975.

*Kraitchik, Maurice. *Mathematical Recreations.* New York: Dover, 1953.

*Lumpkin, Beatrice & Dorothy Strong. *Multicultural Math and Science Connections.* Portland, ME: J. Weston Walch, 1995.

*McConville, Robert. *A History of Board Games.* Palo Alto, CA: Creative Publications, 1974.

National Council of Teachers of Mathematics. *Principles and Standards for School Mathematics.* Reston, VA: NCTM, 2000. (Also see the NCTM series of edited volumes on gender and various cultures: *Changing the Faces of Mathematics.*)

Nelson, David, George G. Joseph & Julian Williams. *Multicultural Mathematics: Teaching Mathematics from a Global Perspective.* Oxford and New York: Oxford University Press, 1993.

*Indicates references used for this book.

*Russ, Larry. *Complete Mancala Games Book.* New York: Marlowe, 2000.

Smith, Jacquelin. "Links to Literature: Threading Mathematics into Social Studies." *Teaching Children Mathematics* Vol. 1 (March 1995): pp. 438–444.

*Whitin, David J. & Sandra Wilde. *Read Any Good Math Lately?* Portsmouth, NH: Heinemann, 1992.

———. *It's the Story That Counts.* Portsmouth, NH: Heinemann, 1995.

*Williams, Geoffrey. *African Designs from Traditional Sources.* New York: Dover, 1971.

*Zaslavsky, Claudia. *Africa Counts: Number and Pattern in African Cultures.* Chicago: Chicago Review Press, 1973, 1999.

*———. *The Multicultural Math Classroom: Bringing in the World.* Portsmouth, NH: Heinemann, 1996.

*———. *Multicultural Mathematics: Interdisciplinary, Cooperative-Learning Activities.* Portland, ME: J. Weston Walch, 1993.

*———. *Multicultural Math: Hands-On Activities from Around the World.* New York: Scholastic Professional, 1994.

*———. "Symmetry in American Folk Art." *Arithmetic Teacher* Vol. 38 (September 1990): pp. 6–12.

*———. *Tic Tac Toe and Other Three-in-a-Row Games.* New York: Crowell, 1982.

*Zhang, Wei. *Exploring Math through Puzzles.* Berkeley: Key Curriculum Press, 1996.


*Indicates references used for this book.

## BOOKS FOR KIDS

ABC Quilts. *Kids Making Quilts for Kids.* Gualala, CA: The Quilt Digest Press, 1992.

Bateson-Hill, Margaret. *Shota and the Star Quilt.* New York: Zero to Ten, Ltd., 1998.

Blood, Charles & Martin Link. *The Goat in the Rug.* New York: Macmillan, 1990.

Bolton, Janet. *My Grandmother's Patchwork Quilt.* New York: Bantam Doubleday Dell, 1994.

Bruchac, Joseph & Jonathan London. *Thirteen Moons on Turtle's Back.* New York: Philomel, 1992.

Caduto, Michael & Joseph Bruchac. *Keepers of the Earth.* New York: Fulcrum, 1988.

Carlson, Laurie. *More Than Moccasins: A Kid's Activity Guide to Traditional North American Indian Life.* Chicago: Chicago Review Press, 1994.

Cobb, Mary. *The Quilt-Block History of Pioneer Days, with Projects Kids Can Make.* Brookfield, CT: The Millbrook Press, 1995.

Earthworks Group. *Fifty Simple Things Kids Can Do To Save the Earth.* Kansas City, MO: Andrews & McMeel, 1990.

Flournoy, Valerie. *The Patchwork Quilt.* New York: Dutton, 1985.

Friedman, Aileen. *A Cloak for the Dreamer.* New York: Scholastic, 1994.

Gerdes, Paulus. *Desenhos da Africa.* São Paulo, Brazil, SP: Editora Scipione, 1990.

Hopkinson, Deborah. *Sweet Clara and the Freedom Quilt.* New York: Knopf, 1993.

Hunt, W. Ben. *Indian Crafts and Lore.* New York: Western Publishing Company, 1954.

Kohl, Herbert. *Insides, Outsides, Loops, and Lines.* New York: Freeman, 1995.

Mendez, Philip. *The Black Snowman.* New York: Scholastic Hardcover, 1989.

Mobley, Chuck & Andrea Mobley. *Navajo Rugs and Blankets: A Coloring Book.* Tucson, AZ: Treasure Chest Publications, 1994.

Paul, Ann Whitford. *Eight Hands Round: A Patchwork Alphabet.* New York: HarperCollins, 1991.

———. *The Seasons Sewn: A Year in Patchwork.* New York: Harcourt Brace, 1996.

Ringgold, Faith. *Tar Beach.* New York: Scholastic, 1991.

Wright, Courtni C. *Jumping the Broom.* New York: Holiday House, 1994. (A star-pattern quilt story.)

Zaslavsky, Claudia. *Math Games and Activities from Around the World.* Chicago: Chicago Review Press, 1998.

———. *Number Sense and Nonsense.* Chicago: Chicago Review Press, 2001.

———. *Tic Tac Toe and Other Three-in-a-Row Games.* New York: Crowell, 1982.

# ALIGNMENT WITH THE NATIONAL COUNCIL OF TEACHERS OF MATHEMATICS 2000 STANDARDS AND OTHER SUBJECTS IN THE CURRICULUM

*Content Standards*
N = Number and Operations
A = Algebra
G = Geometry
M = Measurement
D = Data Analysis and Probability

*Process Standards*
P = Problem Solving
R = Reasoning and Proof
C = Communication
CN = Connection
RP = Representation

*Subject Matter Alignment*
L = Language Arts
S = Social Studies
F = Fine Arts
SC = Science

## 1. Three-in-a-Row Games

| | N | A | G | M | D | P | R | C | CN | RP | L | S | F | SC |
|---|---|---|---|---|---|---|---|---|---|---|---|---|---|---|
| Nine Holes, from England (p. 4) | | | • | • | | • | • | • | | | • | • | • | |
| Tic-Tac-Toe (p. 8) | | | • | | | • | • | • | | | • | • | | |
| Magic Square Tic-Tac-Toe, from Ancient China (p. 11) | • | | • | • | | • | • | • | • | | • | | | |
| Number Tic-Tac-Toe (p. 13) | • | | • | | | • | • | • | | | | | | |
| Achi, from Ghana (p. 14) | | | • | • | | • | • | • | | | | | | |
| Six Men's Morris, from Italy, France, and England (p. 16) | | | • | | | • | • | • | • | | • | • | | |
| Alquerque de Nueve, from Spain (p. 18) | | | • | • | | • | • | • | • | | • | • | • | |
| Jirig, from Mongolia (p. 21) | | | • | • | | • | • | • | • | | • | | | |
| Murabaraba, from Lesotho and South Africa (p. 23) | | | • | • | | • | • | • | • | | • | | | |
| The Shape of the Game Board (p. 26) | • | | • | • | | • | • | | • | | • | | | |

## 2. More Board Games

| | N | A | G | M | D | P | R | C | CN | RP | L | S | F | SC |
|---|---|---|---|---|---|---|---|---|---|---|---|---|---|---|
| Leopards and Tigers, from Thailand (p. 29) | | | • | | | • | • | • | • | | • | | | |
| Lambs and Tigers, from India (p. 31) | | | • | | | • | • | • | • | | • | | | |
| Tchuka Ruma, from Indonesia (p. 33) | | | • | • | | • | • | • | | | • | • | | |
| Little Goat Game, from Sudan (p. 35) | | | • | • | | • | • | • | | | • | | | |
| Cow Game, from Sudan (p. 37) | | | • | • | | • | • | • | | | • | • | | |
| Adi, from Ghana (p. 39) | | | | | | • | • | • | • | | • | • | | |

## 3. How People Use Numbers

| | N | A | G | M | D | P | R | C | CN | RP | L | S | F | SC |
|---|---|---|---|---|---|---|---|---|---|---|---|---|---|---|
| The Abacus, from Russia (p. 43) | • | • | | • | | • | • | • | • | | • | | | |
| The Abacus, from China (p. 45) | • | • | | • | | • | • | • | | | • | | | |
| The Calendar of the Iroquois of North America (p. 47) | • | • | | | | • | • | • | | | • | • | • | • |
| The Calendar of the Maya, from Mexico and Central America (p. 49) | • | • | | | | • | • | • | | | • | • | | • |
| Signs of the Zodiac, from China (p. 51) | • | | • | • | • | | • | • | • | | • | • | • | • |
| Wampum, Cocoa Beans, and Pieces of Eight, from the American Colonies (p. 53) | • | | | | | | • | • | | | • | • | | |
| Beads, Shells, and Gold, from Africa (p. 56) | • | | | | | | • | • | • | | • | | | |
| Save Those Cans! from the United States (p. 58) | • | • | | | | • | • | • | • | • | • | • | | • |
| Saving the Lives of Children Throughout the World (p. 60) | • | | | | | | • | • | • | | • | | | • |

### 4. Is There a Lucky Number?

| | N | A | G | M | D | P | R | C | CN | RP | L | S | F | SC |
|---|---|---|---|---|---|---|---|---|---|---|---|---|---|---|
| Thirteen—Lucky or Unlucky? from the United States (p. 63) | | | | | | • | • | • | | | • | • | | |
| Seven—Lucky or Unlucky? from the Ancient World (p. 65) | • | | | | | • | • | • | | | • | • | | • |
| Letters and Numbers, from Europe (p. 68) | • | | | | | • | • | • | • | | • | | | |
| Magic Squares, from China and the Muslim World (p. 70) | • | • | • | | | • | • | • | | | • | | | |
| Playing with Magic Squares, for Everybody (p. 72) | • | • | • | | | • | • | • | | | • | | | |
| Four-by-Four Magic Squares, from Europe (p. 74) | • | • | • | | | • | • | • | | | • | | • | |
| Panmagic Magic Squares (p. 76) | • | • | • | | | • | • | • | | • | | | | |

### 5. How People Measure

| | N | A | G | M | D | P | R | C | CN | RP | L | S | F | SC |
|---|---|---|---|---|---|---|---|---|---|---|---|---|---|---|
| Standard Measures, from Ancient Rome (p. 79) | • | | | • | • | • | • | • | | | • | • | | • |
| Standard Measures, from Ancient Egypt (p. 81) | • | • | | • | | • | | • | • | | • | • | | • |
| Log Cabin, from the United States (p. 82) | • | • | • | • | | • | | • | • | | • | | | |
| The Iroquois Longhouse, from New York State and Canada (p. 84) | • | • | • | • | | • | | • | • | • | • | | | |
| Panpipes, from South America (p. 86) | • | | | • | • | | | • | | | • | • | • | |
| Save the Water, for the World (p. 88) | • | | | • | • | • | • | • | | | • | | | • |

### 6. Puzzles with Dots, String, and Paper Strips

| | N | A | G | M | D | P | R | C | CN | RP | L | S | F | SC |
|---|---|---|---|---|---|---|---|---|---|---|---|---|---|---|
| Julirde, from West Africa (p. 91) | | | • | | | • | • | • | | | • | | | |
| Bead and String Puzzle, from China and West Africa (p. 94) | | | • | • | | • | • | • | | | • | | | |
| Möbius Strip Surprises, from Germany (p. 96) | • | | • | • | | • | | • | | | • | • | | |
| Sand Drawings I: Animal Pictures, from Angola, Africa (p. 98) | | | • | | | • | • | • | | | • | | | |
| Sand Drawings II: The Story of Three Villages, from Angola (p. 102) | | | • | | | • | • | • | | | • | • | | |
| Sand Drawings III: Welcome to Our Home, from India (p. 104) | | | • | | | • | • | • | | | • | • | | |

### 7. Symmetry and Similarity of Designs

| | N | A | G | M | D | P | R | C | CN | RP | L | S | F | SC |
|---|---|---|---|---|---|---|---|---|---|---|---|---|---|---|
| Native American Beadwork—Part I (p. 108) | • | • | • | | | • | • | • | | | • | • | | |
| Native American Beadwork—Part II (p. 110) | • | • | • | • | | • | • | • | | | • | • | | |
| Native American Painted Designs (p. 112) | • | | • | • | | • | • | • | | | • | • | | |
| Akua Ba Doll, from Ghana (p. 114) | • | | • | • | | • | • | • | | • | • | • | | |
| Our Alphabet, from Ancient Rome (p. 116) | | | • | | | • | • | • | | • | • | | | |
| Flags with Stars, from Many Countries (p. 118) | | | • | • | | • | • | • | | | • | • | | |
| Multiplying Five-Pointed Stars (p. 120) | | | • | • | | • | • | • | | | • | • | | |
| Draw Stars with One Stroke (p. 122) | | | • | • | | • | • | • | | | | • | | |

| | N | A | G | M | D | P | R | C | CN | RP | L | S | F | SC |
|---|---|---|---|---|---|---|---|---|---|---|---|---|---|---|
| Navajo Weaving, from Native America (p. 124) | | | • | • | • | • | | • | • | | • | • | | |
| Star-Patterned Patchwork Quilts, from the United States (p. 127) | | | • | • | • | • | • | • | | | • | • | | |
| More Patchwork Quilt Designs (p. 130) | | | • | • | • | • | | • | | | • | • | | |

| 8. Repeated Patterns | N | A | G | M | D | P | R | C | CN | RP | L | S | F | SC |
|---|---|---|---|---|---|---|---|---|---|---|---|---|---|---|
| Embroidery, from Hungary (p. 133) | | | • | • | • | | | • | | | • | • | | |
| Tessellations—Repeating the Design (p. 135) | | | • | • | • | | | | | • | | • | | |
| Adire Cloth, from Nigeria (p. 138) | | | • | • | • | | | • | | | • | • | | |
| Sashiko Embroidery, from Japan—Part I (p. 140) | | | • | • | • | | | • | | | • | • | | |
| Sashiko Embroidery, from Japan—Part II (p. 142) | | | • | • | • | | | • | | | • | • | | |
| Islamic Art, from Spain (p. 143) | | | • | • | • | | | • | | | • | • | | |
| Islamic Art, from Iran (formerly Persia) (p. 146) | | | • | • | • | | | • | | | • | • | | |
| Fractal Patterns, from Native North America (p. 148) | | | • | • | • | | | • | | | • | • | | |

# *Also* by Claudia Zaslavsky

## Math Games and Activities from Around the World
Ages 9 & up

"A splendidly sneaky way of countering math anxiety."

—*Hungry Mind Review*

"If I were to buy only one resource to provide myriad activities throughout the school year, I would choose this book."

—*Mathematics Teaching in the Middle School*

"This book is a treasure trove of multicultural information and fun."

—*Children's Literature Newsletter*

More than 70 math games, puzzles, and projects from all over the world encourage kids to hone their math skills as they use geometry to design game boards, probability to analyze the outcomes of games of chance, and logical thinking to devise strategies for the games.

Illustrated throughout
1-55652-287-8
$14.95 (CAN $22.95)

## Number Sense and Nonsense
Building Math Creativity and Confidence Through Number Play
Ages 8 & up

"An innovative approach to teaching the properties and relationship of numbers and their relevance in the everyday world."

—*School Library Journal*

"*Number Sense and Nonsense* is a wonderful book for any upper elementary or middle school teacher."

—*Teaching Children Mathematics*

"Written in an easy style that both entertains and instructs . . . a wonderful resource for mathematics teachers to have within easy reach."

—*Mathematics Teaching in the Middle School*

More than 80 group and individual games and activities teach fun, useful ways to manipulate odd and even numbers; prime and composite numbers; factors, divisors, and multiples of numbers; and common and decimal fractions. Counting, calculating, and writing numbers in cultures from China and Egypt to Native America provide more practice in understanding how numbers work. Riddles, puzzles, number tricks, and calculator games boost estimating and computation skills for every math student.

Illustrated throughout
1-55652-378-5
$14.95 (CAN $22.95)

CHICAGO REVIEW PRESS

**Distributed by Independent Publishers Group**
**www.ipgbook.com**
**Available at your local bookstore or**
**order by calling (800) 888-4741.**